W9-CYT-401

20 SEXUALLY ALIVE WOMEN

freely and unashamedly tell their uncensored
stories in this breakthrough book that goes
beyond the stereotypes to bare the total
truth about women who wholeheartedly
acknowledge their sexuality. They are women
who know their bodies and are comfortable with them. And although they refuse
to be bound by all of society's dictates, they
have a personal code of ethics and are
guided not only by desire but by their brains
and their hearts.

SECRETS OF THE
SEXUALLY
ALIVE WOMEN

Ⓢ SIGNET   Ⓜ MENTOR

EXPERT ADVICE

(0451)

☐ **HOW TO BE AN ASSERTIVE (NOT AGGRESSIVE) WOMAN IN LIFE, IN LOVE, AND ON THE JOB—A Total Guide to Self-Assertiveness by Jean Baer.** Are you a portrait of a "lady"—or are you a person? Learn how to express your opinions and wishes, and stand up for your rights with these revolutionary new techniques of assertiveness training by the co-author of the bestselling *Don't Say Yes When You Want to Say No.* (158245—$4.50)

☐ **FOR EACH OTHER: Sharing Sexual Intimacy by Lonnie Barbach.** Every woman longs for greater sexual satisfaction and a more intimate relationship. This famed psychologist and sex therapist gives the program for the aspects of a relationship—physical and psychological— that affect sexual satisfaction. "New discoveries . . . the best book about female sexuality now available."—*Psychology Today* (152719—$4.95)

☐ **FOR YOURSELF: The Fulfillment of Female Sexuality by Lonnie Barbach.** Here is a unique book that demonstrates in a step-by-step program how you can indeed take control of your life at its most intimate, personal and fundamental level—to achieve orgasm and a greater fulfillment of your sexual potential. (159500—$4.50)

☐ **THE TYPE E* WOMAN: How to Overcome the Stress of Being *Everything to Everybody by Harriet B. Braiker, Ph.D.** This insightful and helpful book is for every woman trying to juggle multiple roles, as the majority of women today do. "Will evoke a collective sigh of relief from women who wonder why more is beginning to feel like less." —*Los Angeles Times* (149998—$4.50)

☐ **THE ULTIMATE PLEASURE** *The Secrets of Easily Orgasmic Women* **by Marc and Judith Meshorer.** Foreword by Beverly Whipple, Ph.D., co-author of *The G Spot.* For the first time women who fully enjoy sex tell how they do it. "A creative upbeat approach to sexual joy."—Dr. Irene Kassorla, author of *Go For It* (150953—$4.50)

Prices slightly higher in Canada

Buy them at your local bookstore or use this convenient coupon for ordering.

NEW AMERICAN LIBRARY
P.O. Box 999, Bergenfield, New Jersey 07621

Please send me the books I have checked above. I am enclosing $_____
(please add $1.00 to this order to cover postage and handling). Send check or money order—no cash or C.O.D.'s. Prices and numbers are subject to change without notice.

Name_____

Address_____

City _____ State _____ Zip Code _____

Allow 4-6 weeks for delivery.

This offer, prices and numbers are subject to change without notice.

SECRETS OF THE SEXUALLY ALIVE WOMAN

(formerly titled
The Sexually Aggressive Woman)

Adelaide Bry

A SIGNET BOOK

NEW AMERICAN LIBRARY

NAL BOOKS ARE AVAILABLE AT QUANTITY DISCOUNTS WHEN USED
TO PROMOTE PRODUCTS OR SERVICES. FOR INFORMATION PLEASE
WRITE TO PREMIUM MARKETING DIVISION, NEW AMERICAN LIBRARY,
1633 BROADWAY, NEW YORK, NEW YORK 10019.

Copyright © 1975 by Adelaide Bry
All rights reserved, including the right to reproduce this book or parts
thereof, in any form, except for the inclusion of brief quotations in a
review. For information address David McKay Company, Inc., a subsidiary
of Random House Company, Inc., 201 East 50 Street, New York,
New York 10022.

This is an authorized reprint of a hardcover edition, entitled
The Sexually Aggressive Woman, published by
a division of David McKay Company, Inc.

SIGNET TRADEMARK REG. U.S. PAT. OFF. AND FOREIGN COUNTRIES
REGISTERED TRADEMARK—MARCA REGISTRADA
HECHO EN DRESDEN, TN, USA

SIGNET, SIGNET CLASSIC, MENTOR, ONYX, PLUME, MERIDIAN
and NAL BOOKS are published by NAL PENGUIN INC.,
1633 Broadway, New York, New York 10019

First Signet Printing, February, 1976

9 10 11 12 13 14 15 16 17

PRINTED IN THE UNITED STATES OF AMERICA

*To women who search
for selfhood in many ways*

Acknowledgments

Special thanks to Maureen Chapman, Gwen Gunn, and George J. Thomson

Contents

A New Note about the Sexually Aggressive Woman

When this book first came out, the phrase "sexually aggressive woman," touched off fireworks. Some men, and women too, looked upon her with disdain, called her "kooky" and "unfeminine."

Others congratulated me on telling her story, saying, in effect, "Thanks for telling the truth, it's been hidden too long."

More truth about women and their sexual behavior has recently been revealed by *Redbook*'s survey of 100,000 women, the most complete survey since the Kinsey Report.

The essence of this excellent report is that, indeed, times have changed, and women are freer. While *Redbook* has no precise category for the "sexually aggressive woman," the survey does show that many American women are well on their way to becoming just that.

Some of the findings I found especially noteworthy are:

- 9 out of 10 women (of the 100,000 surveyed) take an active role in sex at least half the time . . . regardless of age, education, income, or religious belief.
- The sexually passive woman is extremely rare these days, not even 1 out of 100.

- Considerable numbers of women engage in sex outside of marriage, while maintaining that their marriage and marital sex are both satisfactory. (See the stories of Joyce and Annette.)
- Women without husbands—single, widowed, or divorced women—are more "assertive." "Assertive" is *Redbook*'s word. (See the stories of Betsey, Edith, Sharon.)
- Oral-genital sex, taboo at the time of the Kinsey Report, is now practiced by 91 percent of women between the ages of 21 and 39.
- 88 out of 100 women who discuss intimate feelings with their husbands also enjoy good sex lives.

When Kinsey concluded in 1953 that women were just as sexual as men, finding the same response to sexual stimulation, that was news. Today the realization that women are living that truth, accepting and expressing their sexuality in ways that their mothers and grandmothers hardly dared to think about, is still newsworthy but hardly shocking.

Yet the sexually aggressive woman is still one step ahead of her sisters; *Redbook*'s final question tells the story. Would you object if your sons engage in premarital sex? The answer—12 percent would object. Would you object if your daughters engage in premarital sex? The answer—24 percent would object.

Even the liberated women of the 1970s still do not *fully* accept their right to their sexuality.

The sexually aggressive woman does.

Introduction

IS IT GOOD OR BAD?

From time to time during the last couple of years I'd heard about an occasionally met women who I would define as being "sexually aggressive." I was, and still am, fascinated, which is why I wanted to know more about these women, and, ultimately, to write this book.

But can one just go out and stand around on street corners, or collar likely-looking females at parties, and say, "Hey, are you a sexually aggressive woman?" Hardly. Or, at least *I* can't.

So, to gather material, I came up with the idea of advertising. I went to several college campuses and posted notices in bookstores, student lounges, and other likely locations. I placed tiny ads in the "personals" columns of a few big-city newspapers and also in two or three dailies serving small- to medium-size communites. I even braved the personnel managers of several large corporations (this was hardest to do) and got permission to tack my neatly typed notices on the bulletin boards in or near the women's lounges.

With minor variations, my ads went something like this: "Psychologist, gathering material for book, seeks interviews with sexually aggressive women." At first I offered $20 per interview, but the response was so staggering that I found myself in real danger of going broke. So I revised the ads, offering no payment in return for the interview. The replies continued to flood in from women who had no difficulty identifying themselves as "sexually aggressive."

Primarily, this book is my selection of tape-recorded interviews with the respondents. Each woman was invited to explain why she considers herself "sexually aggressive"; otherwise, I asked no standard questions. Where the interviews are edited, it is for the sake of clarity and to avoid redundancy.

The women I spoke with range in age from eighteen to fifty-five. Some are single, some are married, some are divorced or widowed. They grew up in happy homes, broken homes, religious homes, and non-religious homes; almost every socioeconomic level is represented.

Not all of these women are aggressive in the same manner or to the same degree. Some are huntresses, "always on the prowl," as one interviewee described herself. For others, aggressiveness is a simple matter (relatively speaking) of demanding and receiving gratification from their own husbands. The one common denominator seems to be that each has acknowledged her own sexual desires and has given herself permission to express them.

Taking the group as a whole, what are these women really like? They did appear to me to be more happy, more outgoing, and more successful than most. There are neurotics among them, as one would expect to find in any group. That their sexual

aggressiveness bears any relation to their neuroti-
cism—or that it is an expression of it—is possible in a
few instances. But I am more than ever convinced
that sexual aggressiveness, unlike its opposite, sexual
repression, is not conducive to neurosis. Just about
anything that frees the inner woman, enabling a full-
er expression of herself, must be considered desirable.

Finally, I want to emphasize that none of these
women is, or ever has been, a patient of mine.

1974   ADELAIDE BRY

Chapter 1

THE SEXUALLY AGGRESSIVE WOMAN: PAST, PRESENT, FUTURE

Perhaps you remember the classic old Tabu perfume ad, the one showing a handsome violinist, overcome by sudden desire, as he gathers his swooning female piano accompanist up into a torrid embrace that literally lifts her off the piano stool.

Perhaps you have also seen a newer version of the same ad. Now the roles are reversed: this time, the violinist is a woman, and now it is she who, prompted by uncontrollable passion, impetuously embraces her compliant *male* accompanist. (It is unclear from the picture whether she is actually lifting him off the piano stool or whether he has half-risen to meet her.)

The ad's headline reads: "Never mind how it happens, it happens."

A gleeful whoop and an "It's about time" were my own first reactions to the ad. True, there is a decidedly tongue-in-cheek quality about the presentation. True, we're not supposed to take it *too* seriously; real women don't ordinarily go around kissing men right out of their piano seats. But it's doubtful that even the most daring and imaginative ad-makers would have proposed the concept ten, even five years ago. Too far out. No one would get it.

We get it today. The ad-makers—who are a very smart bunch, let's not forget—know that somewhere deep in our collective consciousness we are ready (however reluctantly and with whatever sense of the impropriety, the absurdity, the sheer outrageousness of the idea) to acknowledge the possibility that some women do, or might want to, assume the role of sexual aggressor.

The sexually aggressive woman is, in fact, alive and well and living among us in greater numbers than one might at first suspect. She is still, however, a partial alien to our culture; we have no very good frame of reference from which to view her. She's a puzzle; we don't quite know what to think of her.

Not so with the sexually aggressive man. The term is self-explanatory—a redundancy in fact. How else, after all, should the normal male express his sexuality but actively, in a confident, persuasive unhung-up, *aggressive* way?

Fucking is, traditionally, a man's game. Women, again according to traditional thinking, can take their sex or leave it. So one wonders: what about the woman who actually goes out looking for it? What kind of creature could she possibly be? Dragon Lady? Vamp? Hip-swiveling Mae Westian caricature? Or—a more contemporary image—sequin—t-shirted, platform-shod groupie, lusting after her rock-star-hero-of-the-moment?

The truth is, although she might bear some slight incidental resemblance to any of these, the sexually aggressive woman is much less a type than she is a healthy, strong personality who has taken it upon herself to define her own sexuality rather than allowing some man, or men, or the society at large to define it for her. She is the woman who acknowledges her own needs and wants—whatever they may be—and then arranges to have them satisfied.

A while back I said that the sexually aggressive woman is a partial alien to our culture because she has no historical precedent. But she may have *pre*historical antecedents. Though it's not my purpose to write a history of female sexuality, it's certainly worth noting that there is a theory—and one that is rapidly gaining acceptance—that long before the Victorians, long before the Egyptians, in fact long before humankind had advanced to a state of anything resembling civilization, the ordinary female of the species was indeed sexually aggressive.

Consider the evidence: though the penis itself is bigger and *looks* more imposing than the clitoris, a woman's pelvic area is supplied with a far greater amount of underlying sexual tissue than a man's— and the more sexually active the woman, the more sensitive and responsive to stimuli this tissue becomes. Research by Masters and Johnson indicates that woman's capacity for orgasm far exceeds the male's. Anthropologists report that even today the women in some primitive societies exhibit a significantly greater appetite for sex than the men. And Mary Jane Sherfey, in her study, *The Nature and Evolution of Female Sexuality*, published by Random House in 1972, speculates that women, if freed from cultural restraint, might be expected to behave similarly to our close relatives, the higher primates—the females of which have been known to copulate as often as fifty times a day when in heat.

Apparently, woman—unrepressed and in her natural or "unacculturated" state—is endowed with an almost limitless capacity for sexual enjoyment. Much has been written explaining how the advent of civilization resulted—or, according to some theories, actually depended upon—the taming of woman's sexuality. I leave it to the interested reader to seek out the material (Dr. Sherfey's study is excellent). The point I wish to make is simply that the sexually aggressive woman, though not the norm in *our* society, is probably not a deviant at all. She may be, instead, the most natural and authentic of females.

After centuries of repression, she reappears in greater numbers now because of a fortunate (or unfortunate, depending on how one reacts to the idea of woman assuming charge of her own sexuality) confluence of trends and events.

First, there is the overall freeing up of society, what has been called "the sexual revolution," which some date from the widespread use of the Pill, others from the coming-of-age of the first Dr. Spock generation of the 1940s. No matter; it has affected almost everyone, and I do not feel compelled to trot out reams of documentation to verify the obvious: an awful lot of men and women are admitting to an awful lot more interest in sex than they used to.

Premarital and extramarital sex, although not exactly officially sanctioned, now raise very few eyebrows except, perhaps, the ones belonging to the parents or spouses of the parties involved. Nudity has lost much of its shock value unless the unclothed person is either very famous and/or very unattractive, and magazines like *Playgirl* and *Viva*, featuring nude male centerfolds, have taken their place on the newsstands alongside *Playboy, Penthouse*, and the like. It is the rare young novelist or playwright who hesitates to sprinkle his/her work with words like "fuck," "prick" and "cunt." (Isadora Wing, the heroine of Erica Jong's novel, *Fear of Flying*, refers to her own cunt in the most offhand way imaginable. It does not jar. No other word would do.) And even the very nicest married ladies—the *Redbook* young mother types—are concerned about their orgasms (clitoral? vaginal? multiple? none?) and consider the matter fit for explicit cocktail party discussion. I know. I've heard them.

And then, of course, there is the women's movement. Each of us, women *and* men, has had his or her consciousness raised, if only by a few fractions of an inch, by its presence and rhetoric, and one need not be in total sympathy with all its aims in order to be deeply affected by its simplest, most basic plea: equal opportunity and freedom of choice for both sexes.

Finally, there is something called the human growth movement. Which is not a movement at all in the sense that women's liberation, with its organized attempts to overhaul the entire political and social structure, is a movement.

Loosely defined, the human growth movement is the synthesis of a group of more or less related psychoanalytic theories, transformed into a variety of therapies, all of which encourage a turning-away from the repressive, alienating, and authoritarian elements in the society, the better to cultivate a capacity for joyous, free, loving, creative, spontaneous existence. But one need never join an encounter group, make the trek to Esalen, or have even the remotest acquaintance with the tenets of transactional analysis to be influenced by the movement. Its injunctions are everywhere and have been taken up with a vengeance by the mass media. In books, magazines, and from the TV screen we are urged by one pop sociologist after another to "experience," to "grow," to "live our lives to the fullest." The effect is cumulative. The word "duty" has fallen into disrepute (unless we are talking about our duty to ourselves), Quite possibly, at no other time in history have so many people been so caught up with the idea of personal freedom.

Put them all together—the sexual revolution; the women's movement, with its emphasis on equality and freedom of choice; and the human growth movement, all urging us on to more joyous, creative lifestyles—and the stage is set for the (re)emergence of the sexually aggressive women.

I think we must assume that the sexually aggressive woman is more than just the product of new trends and changing attitudes, though certainly she has been mightily influenced by them. I think we must view her as a rather special woman. She is sensitive to social change, but, even more important, she is so psychically constituted that she has managed to grow up whole. And she has a keen sense of herself as a powerful sexual being at a time when other women remain "female eunuchs" (as Germaine Greer aptly expressed it), perhaps aware of options but nevertheless locked into patterns that render them powerless.

We do not know why one woman assumes power while another does not, just as we cannot say for sure why one person matures into healthy, self-assertive adulthood, often despite overwhelmingly adverse circumstances, while another, seemingly more favored, grows up guilt-ridden and emotionally maimed. There are theories, of course, but the mystery still has not been solved to the satisfaction of most. When it is, we psychologists may be able to write behavioral prescriptions for maladies of the psyche with the same confidence with which doctors of medicine now select drugs for sickness of the body.

Power, it appears, is the name of the game for the sexually aggressive woman, and it is this sense of her own power, fed by strong feelings of self-worth, that enables her to make what she will of sex.

I think it's important to make a distinction here between the positive power claimed by the sexually aggressive woman and the negative power exercised by the more conventional woman.

It can be argued that *all* women, even the sexually conservative, have power in the sense that they can, if they wish, barter their favors in return for money or special privileges, or withhold them in order to get and keep a man. But the sexually conservative woman, and even the sexually cooperative woman, are passive, or "done-to," parties in any sexual encounter.

The sexually cooperative woman, an interesting phenomenon in her own right, appeared in the Fifties and Sixties. She is what the sexual revolution was all about. The entire trend, in fact, was predicated on her "yes" answers—her simple willingness to participate. She may enjoy sex and even go out of her way to make herself available, but—and here is where she differs from the sexually aggressive woman—she neither expects nor demands that her own needs be met. Orgasm, for example, is delightful (as it is for *anyone*), but she does not consider it an inalienable right and is not above faking it in order to please a lover.

By contrast, the sexually aggressive woman is a "do-er." She not only often makes the initial approach; she is also an equal or dominant participant in the sex act itself and does not hesitate to indicate, either verbally or otherwise, what she wants from her partner.

It's possible that the sexually aggressive woman even enjoys sex more than her more traditional counterparts. Psychologist Abraham Maslow's study,* in which passive femininity is contrasted with the qualities of the so-called dominant woman, seems to bear this out. ("Dominant" is Maslow's term, but I think we may fairly substitute the word "aggressive.")

Maslow discovered that the more dominant the woman, the more profound her sexual pleasure. "Our analysis of sexuality and dominance has shown

* Abraham Maslow "Dominance, Personality, and Social Behavior in Women," Journal of Social Psychology, Vol. 10, 1939. 3-39.

that dominance feeling and sexual attitude are very highly correlated. ... the woman rated high in sexual attitude accepts everything: promiscuity, homosexuality, masturbation . . . cunnilingus, fellatio, and experimentation of every conceivable kind. It would seem as if every sexual impulse or desire ... may emerge freely and without inhibition in these [dominant] women."*

And what *about* guilt? The sexually aggressive women whose interviews are included in this book appear to be remarkably guilt-free. Most do not even use the word in connection with their activities. The ones who do often mention it as something they have managed to overcome. In any case, regardless of whether or not they are acquainted with Freudian thought, they seem to have adopted the Freudian belief that guilt is only related to what has been learned—and therefore can be unlearned—and that there is no larger Godlike presence lurking in the wings, waiting to strike them down because of unconventional sexual activity.

The sexually aggressive woman—always with individual differences—can be further characterized by some or all of the following traits and attitudes.

• She is usually capable of forming strong attachments, but, unlike many other women, she is not content to live vicariously.

• She is neither a masochist nor a martyr. She seeks pleasure and views the gratification of her own desires as being at least as important as gratifying the desires of others.

* Abraham Maslow, Ibid., pp. 33.

• She refuses to be bound by the sexual dictates of the culture, her religion, her family, and/or the men in her life. Instead, she operates according to a personal code of ethics. Casual sex with strangers, extramarital sex, bisexual encounters, group sex, "kinky" sex—all are permissible or not, depending on the personal morality she has adopted. Which morality, in turn, is based on the premise that if *she* enjoys it, if it makes *her* feel good, then it's okay.

She knows her body in a way that many more conventional women do not. Many masturbate more or less frequently. Some have experimented on themselves with vibrators. Others reported studying their vaginal areas with mirrors. (To paraphrase one interviewee: "There's a whole world down there under the pubic hair, and many women don't even know what it looks like.")

Perhaps because she's so well-acquainted with her own body, she is highly aware of how she responds to various kinds of sexual stimuli and she makes certain she gets the message across to her partner. She knows exactly how she wants her breasts caressed, her clitoris manipulated. (One woman was able to specify the distinctly different sensations she experienced when different "corners" of her vagina were touched, licked, or sucked.)

She is also comfortable with the *appearance* of her body. Although our culture places a high premium on youth and beauty, none of these women seemed greatly concerned by physical imperfections—certainly not in the neurotic sense that sends some women into deep depression at the first evidence of physical decline.

Though some are especially attractive, only one or two of the sexually aggressive women I spoke with are beautiful in the conventional sense. Some are decidedly overweight; some have disproportionately large (or small) hips and/or breasts; some have complexion problems. The older ones have their fair share of wrinkles and sagging flesh. Nevertheless, very few indicated dissatisfaction with their physical appearance; on the contrary, they exuded pride and confidence in their bodies. They assumed that they are attractive to men simply by virtue of their being female and *alive*.

The sexually aggressive woman is willing to take risks and is courageous enough to face up to the consequences of her actions. She runs the risk of relatively frequent rejection, for example. Not all men are turned on by her advances. Some back away politely, murmuring chivalrous refusals. Others, offended or incensed by her approach (interpreted as trespassing on *their* turf) are more brutal. She can cope.

In fact, she exhibits a number of traits which in our culture are traditionally associated with masculinity. She is more often active rather than passive, independent rather than dependent, assertive rather than weak-willed, venturesome rather than timid, forthright rather than devious.

I think it's possible to make too much of this last quality and to interpret it as a conscious (or subconscious) desire to abdicate womanliness in favor of being "like men." I see it otherwise. Passive, dependent, weak-willed, timid, devious people of either sex are far less likely to lead rich and interesting lives than are active, independent, assertive, venturesome, forthright people (again, of either sex), and women who display the latter qualities are not so much acting "like men" as they are functioning as strong, vibrant human beings.

The sexually aggressive woman is not the average or the norm. She may be just a few in number. But she sets an example. Her sisters can learn from her, just as they are learning new modes of behavior from *other* adventurous women who are stepping forward to assert themselves in *other* areas. Through her example, perhaps the time will come when all women will feel free enough to express their sexuality as openly and, yes, as aggressively as most men do today.

Good sex is only one part of the good life. But it is far too important for any of us just to sit back and wait for it to happen.

Chapter 2

WIVES AND MOTHERS

There she is: Mrs. America. Scrubbed. Shiny. Santized. Just like her kitchen sink. But *nice*. A giving person, not a taker. Living for and through her husband and children. And so concerned with *their* happiness and well-being, one doubts she has the impulse, let alone the time and energy, to invest in any benefits for her own self.

A one-dimensional picture, yes. Chances are there never really was such a woman. But the mythic image persists, maybe because it's so reassuring. (Mom's in the kitchen . . . all's right with the world.) In any case, vast numbers of people continue to cling to it, and the ones who do are inclined to feel there's something, well, if not absolutely wrong, then at least not quite right about the woman who doesn't at least make an effort to conform to it.

The trouble is—and it's always been a problem, though certainly we're hearing more about it now than ever before—that some women who have chosen to be wives and mothers don't feel comfortable living selflessly, within the conventional mold. It doesn't fit. It doesn't conform to their own particular psychic construction.

The sexually aggressive woman who is also a wife and mother is one of these. She does not buy the idea that for a married woman, selflessness is its own reward. (Who, after all, would make a similar claim for the married man?) And so she probably focuses less on her husband and children than other wives and mothers do. Many would describe her as selfish.

The irony is that the woman whose whole life does revolve around her family is perhaps even more selfish. She cannot help making demands that are sometimes impossible for others to meet. Since she is dependent on them for *all* forms of her gratification, she may feel resentful when they do not come through for her—when her children don't make straight A's in school, for example. Or when her husband doesn't out-earn the guy next door. Or supply her with enough orgasms. The woman whose well-developed sense of self doesn't allow for total submersion in anyone else's life, who takes responsibility for gratifying some of her own desires—either through her work, or sexually, or otherwise—exerts far less pressure on her family to perform. As a result, everyone is happier.

Because of the circumstances of her life, the sexually aggressive woman who is also a wife and mother is less able than others to exercise erotic options. Her time, her privacy, her energy are subject to the demands made by her family. Unless she and her husband are both feminists, it is she who runs their home and cares for their children, and, in this sense, she remains the giver in the relationship. But, like other sexually aggressive women, she demands an equal give-and-take in the sexual sphere. If she is able to obtain the gratification she seeks solely through her husband, she may be among the most happily married of all women. For her, monogamy is not a bore, or a chore, or a sacrifice. It is a feast and a delight.

For some other married women—even those with very deep feelings of caring and affection for their husbands (and a commitment to the institution of marriage)—one man simply is not enough. Such women must choose between a life of frustration—or one or more extramarital affairs. The true sexually aggressive woman opts for the latter.

For her, conventional morality is beside the point. One woman I spoke with justified her behavior with the following analogy (admittedly a bit strained): "If you're very hungry you don't stop to consider the ethics of stealing a piece of bread. If you're starved for sex, fidelity is a meaningless concept."

Most of these women are notable in their ability to separate sex from love—or, at any rate, extramarital sex from the friendly, loving feelings they have for their husbands. No doubt they can do this because, like many men but unlike many women, they wholeheartedly acknowledge their sexuality.

The woman who cannot accept her own sex drive (perhaps because somewhere along the line, the culture persuaded her that she doesn't have one) will often convince herself that the lust she feels is really love. Many an unfortunate marriage and many divorces are the result of a confusion between the two.

There is a new tendency among the young, who

look on appalled as the divorce rate continues to climb, to attempt a similar separation between lust and love: between the physical turn-on, on the one hand, and genuine feelings of closeness and caring. Presumably, to be able to do so is to be in a better position to marry "for the right reasons."

Surely, the best marriages draw on elements of both lust and love, and I personally am not convinced that good sex should be discounted as one of the ingredients necessary for happiness in marriage. But it seems to me that these young people are on the right track, and it will be interesting to see what happens to the divorce rate if this attitude becomes widespread.

If we are to believe the social scientists who tell us that the structure of the American marriage is undergoing a gradual change, and I see no reason not to believe them, the sexually aggressive wife and mother is partly responsible for the change. She is one of those who, in different ways and for various reasons, are learning to look upon themselves and their spouses as people—unique, living, breathing individuals with undeniable individual needs and wants that nothing (not even marriage) can cancel out.

Peggy

"I feel no guilt about my other life—my sex life apart from Martin."

A tall woman with sandy-blonde, shoulder-length hair and a fresh complexion, Peggy is twenty-nine and the mother of two pre-schoolers. Martin, her husband, is a research scientist, deeply involved in his work. Their marriage is eight years old.

We talked in the living room of their big, old two-story frame house. Peggy, in blue jeans, sat crosslegged on the sofa, sipping black coffee. She spoke without hesitation, although she told me that she'd never discussed her sexuality before with anyone but Martin and a close friend who is also a psychotherapist.

I suppose I ought to begin at the beginning. At twenty-one, when Martin and I were married, I was a virgin. I used to think of myself as being anti-sex. But that was because I'd never tried it.

The first few times with Martin weren't all that successful. No orgasms. Martin once said that being a virgin so long had refrigerated me!

But it didn't take long for me to warm up and begin to enjoy myself. I discovered my body. I discovered the orgasm. Sex was fun. The best fun I'd ever had.

27

There was a time, oh, maybe a year after our wedding, when I'd keep Martin in bed for *hours*. I found I wanted more than one orgasm per session. But he couldn't last. As soon as he came, he'd lose interest. I also wanted sex every day, but he was often too tired to manage it.

This went on for a while, and it began to be very difficult for both of us. I wasn't satisfied. And he resented my asking for more than he could give.

By the time our first baby was born, we were having long and very serious discussions about divorce. Neither of us really wanted it. We were okay except for the sex thing. We really liked and respected each other as people and we had some marvelous times together. But I couldn't forgive him for not giving me enough sex and he couldn't forgive me for wanting so much.

The solution was obvious, but it took a long time to hit on it. We would stay married, but I would take a lover, or lovers—as many as I needed.

We agreed, though, that I would sleep only with people outside our circle of friends and acquaintances. Strangers. I, personally, could never go to bed with the husband of a friend, and Martin didn't especially like the idea of my having sex with any of the men he knows.

Martin seemed relieved when we came to this decision, and of course I was looking forward to more and better sex. (By that time, there was almost no physical contact between us; Martin avoided me, no doubt because he felt my demands were excessive and he doubted his capacity to meet them.)

But then I had the problem of finding the right

men. It took me a long time to figure a way out of that one. I couldn't go into a bar and pick up a man. I just couldn't. I've always hated the bar scene. I don't even drink. And I'm not very sexy-looking. I dreaded the possibility of approaching someone and then being rejected.

Then one day at a friend's house I was leafing through a literary newspaper. The last two pages were full of classified ads placed by men and women who were looking for sex. Amazing! I read through several of the ads. These people didn't sound like kooks or nuts. Most of them described themselves as graduate students or professional people. Many said they were married.

I went home and composed an ad of my own: "Twenty-nine-year-old mother of two, happily married, intelligent and reasonably attractive, wants discreet extracurricular sex." I used a box number so that I could screen the responses. If there were any.

I got dozens of replies. From businessmen, doctors, teachers, students, most of them also happily married, but, like me, not quite satisfied in the sex department.

One guy sounded perfect: "I'm married, too," he wrote. "I have three small kids and I care about my wife. I care about sex, too, but she's always too tired. When can we meet?"

I called him and we made a date for lunch. At a restaurant. We wanted to look each other over before committing ourselves.

The first meeting was awkward. Neither of us had done anything quite like it before. We didn't discuss sex at all—just inflation, our favorite movies, and so on. Anyone listening would have thought we were on a first date. I guess in a way we were.

By the time lunch was over, I'd decided I did want to sleep with Joe. So I said very casually, although I wasn't feeling casual at all, "Tuesday afternoons are good." Joe nodded, kissed me goodbye on the cheek, and said, "Next Tuesday."

Joe came the following Tuesday and we immediately went up to my bedroom. It worked out beautifully.

Having Joe come over once a week—and the anticipation of being with him—gives a new dimension to my life. I feel much less resentment toward Martin. Martin tells me I'm a lot easier to live with now. Even our sex is better, I suppose because he knows it's not all his responsibility anymore. I suspect, too, that he's secretly excited by the idea of my having a lover.

As for Joe, we're a good sex match. I've asked him to suck me for as long as an hour—and he will. Martin never had the patience for that. Joe and I are perfectly free with each other. But we never, ever, discuss our lives, our marriages.

About six months ago, something *very* interesting happened. Martin and I have a good friend who is a psychotherapist. One of his patients, a young man named Gary, had a lot of anxiety about sex. Gary had had a couple of gay experiences, and because of them he was afraid he'd never be able to make it with a woman. He thought he was gay, and he wasn't happy about it.

Dr. R. tried to tell Gary that adolescent homosexuality is pretty common and that one or two encounters don't necessarily mean you're gay for life. He tried to make Gary understand that if he really wanted to, he could have intercourse with a woman. Well . . . Gary did want to, but he was afraid.

Dr. R. was impatient, because traditional conversational therapy wasn't working. Because of Gary's age—he's sixteen—the doctor felt he should experience heterosexual sex *now*. Not five years from now when his perception of himself as gay might be much more firmly fixed. So Dr. R. asked me if I would initiate Gary. Ummmmm. The role of the experienced older woman who initiates young men into the delights of sex! What a challenge! What a beautiful way to use my own experience. And, frankly, what fun! Would I do it? Of course I would! (Martin, by the way, was intrigued with the idea. "Right on," he said.)

Dr. R. gave my phone number to Gary. He was so scared when he called, his voice was just a little whisper. We made a date for an evening when Martin had a meeting.

Gary cancelled out. He cancelled three times. The fourth time he called, I said, "Be here!" Very gently, but it was an *order*.

He showed up, so frightened and embarrassed he couldn't look me in the eye. He was angelic. Long blond hair, the beginnings of a beard, a nice lean sixteen-year-old body.

I put on some records and we had some wine. I wore a black see-through blouse, no bra, and pants with an elastic waistband—easy to get out of.

Dr. R. had warned me to go slow. Otherwise, his fear might take over. So I sat with Gary on the sofa for almost an hour. I held his hand, touched his ear, ruffled his hair. I wanted to let him get used to the feel of me, the smell of me. We talked about music, his schoolwork, his plans for college. I purposely said very little about myself; I felt the more I could stay just a warm body, the better it would be.

After a while, when he had a good strong erection—his jeans bulged—I took his hand, squeezed it, and led him upstairs. He sat down on the bed and waited. Like a child. Very gently, I unbuttoned his shirt, put my arms around him and pulled him down next to me. I kissed his forehead, his cheeks, his ears. I kissed him for a long time on the mouth.

I'd had a good briefing from Dr. R. He told me that Gary often studied pictures of nude women while he masturbated, but that he'd never seen a naked female in the flesh—no pun intended. Now it was time that he did. I stood up, took off my blouse, and slid my pants down. I could almost feel his eyes boring into me when I leaned over to switch on the radio. But when I turned back to him, he was busy picking lint from the bedspread. He was too shy to let me catch him looking.

I sat down on the bed and smiled. He smiled back. We talked some more and in a few minutes I noticed his eyes darting here and there over my body. I have a habit of twisting and curling my pubic hair when I'm nude. I was doing it then and Gary was fascinated. Good, I thought. At least he's getting used to the look of the triangle.

By then I was warming up to my role—feeling like an actress in some wonderful pornographic drama. I was also very turned on.

I unzipped his pants, helped him out of his shirt and shorts. Then I pulled back the covers and we got into bed. No words, but the music from the radio covered the silence.

I pressed up close against him. His penis was so hard, I was afraid he'd come before we started screwing. But I didn't feel we were quite ready for screwing yet. He still hadn't touched me.

I took his hand, cupped it over my breast, and moved it in a circular motion. Then I brought his head down to my other breast and he took the nipple in his mouth.

He fondled my breasts for a while. Then I took one of his hands and placed it on my vagina—which was very wet. I opened the lips and put his fingers in. Next, I showed him my clitoris and how to rub it very lightly back and forth with just the tips of two fingers.

He wasn't afraid anymore. Lust seemed to have taken the place of fear. He began to kiss me very hard and in another minute he was on top of me. I helped him get his penis in and he started to move. It was wild and violent. It took him about thirty seconds to come and that was that. But I could tell he felt pretty good about himself. He had this silly, dopey grin on his face.

As a sexual experience, it wasn't the greatest thing for me. But somehow it was the most total act of giving in my entire life. I had helped a boy to manhood. I've always wondered why Americans are so uncivilized about an initiation ceremony that many a good European parent actually arranges for a son. I suppose today not as many young men need it as before, but Dr. R. feels there will always be a few who do.

Now Dr. R. has another patient, a twenty-one-year-old college boy who has been involved in a homosexual relationship for almost a year. He's scared to death of women and Dr. R. wants me to take the case as "co-therapist." And I will. Imagine it. Me. A virgin at marriage and now a sex therapist!

No, I feel no guilt about my other life—my sex life apart from Martin. I think I might if Martin didn't know the truth about what I do. But he knows everything and he accepts it and in a way even encourages it.

I was miserable before. Resentful and hostile. I blamed Martin for every little thing that went wrong. If I broke a dish it was Martin's fault. Irrational. What I was really reacting to was his less-than-enthusiastic lovemaking. The blame spilled over into everything else.

I don't see what my activities have to do with Martin, anyway. I don't see that they make me less a wife and mother than, say, a woman who might want a lot more sex than her husband can give, but suffers in silence, without doing anything about it. That kind of woman ... well, she's in bad shape and she's probably a bitch to live with. I know. I was there.

Peggy is one of those women whose intense sexuality crept up on her. In effect, it took her by surprise. A virgin on her wedding day, within a year she was keeping Martin in bed for "hours." Consis-

tently she wanted more sex than he could or would provide.

Many women would have settled at this point, experiencing frustration, but ultimately adjusting to the situation. Peggy couldn't. She refused to believe that adjusting was her duty. She and Martin began to contemplate divorce as a final solution.

But Peggy and Martin liked each other. They recognized that though their sexual appetites were incompatible, they, themselves, were not. So they made a joint decision that Peggy would engage in extramarital sex, and it was this that made their marriage feasible.

In order to give up the concept of fidelity, they had to be able to contradict the culture without guilt, and apparently they are able to do so. Their ability to see and deal with life as it is, not as it "should be," is a tribute to both of them.

Peggy has changed enormously since her marriage, moving from a "refrigerated" virgin to a sexually aggressive woman.

When asked to initiate a young man, she is not outraged; instead, she accepts and delights in the opportunity. She sees that particular form of aggressiveness as an act of generosity and kindness.

Joyce

"I will not be bound by anybody's idea of what a woman should or should not do."

At thirty-five, Joyce has been married for seventeen years and is the mother of two boys, eleven and nine. She has a lithe, slender body, dark hair that falls sleek and straight to her shoulders, and a decisive manner of speaking. There is an air of bravado about her. "Gutsy" is the word for Joyce.

She is also very eager to talk. She starts to speak the moment I enter her large, none-too-neat suburban home. I have to ask her to backtrack to get the tape recorder going.

My personal definition of a sexually aggressive woman is one who considers fucking one of the most important things in life, finds it impossible to be without a man, and enjoys the chase. She's a huntress. On the prowl. Most of all, she puts herself on the line. She takes chances. She risks. She's not afraid of being rejected.

I've taken chances. I've been rejected. So okay, it hurts a little bit. I say "what the hell," and I pick myself up and I start all over again. Just like in the song.

Bill—my husband—and I met this couple at a

resort. I knew right away that the guy was my type. A nice, sensitive, easy-going guy, not a ladies' man. Definitely not the kind like the one in the joke where a girl and a guy are on a bus and they keep staring at each other and finally the girl says "Your place or mine?" and then they get off and without saying a word they fuck and that's that. That's not for me.

Anyway, we met this couple and the man was my type. I suggested that the four of us all go out to dinner when we got back to town. I was at the restaurant early, before my husband got there, and I sat next to the guy and I flattered him a little. Told him how great he looked, that kind of thing. Then, while we were eating, I leaned over and whispered "Call me."

He looked at me as though I was a bug in his soup. Shock! I thought, "Oh, well, he's not used to being propositioned. He's probably just being coy." But he never called and we never saw them again as a couple, either. I'd miscalculated.

Not too long ago, I met another guy at the office where I work part-time. I invited him to have lunch. I'd made up my mind to go to bed with him. I told him right out: "You're it. I want you." That's when he told me he'd been making elaborate plans to seduce *me*.

I always tell my men right off, at the beginning. And when it's over, it's over. No scenes. Just good-bye and that's it. You see, I don't fuck just any old body. I don't make it with strangers. I don't want to have to ask afterwards, "What's your name? With whom do I have the pleasure?" But at the same time, I certainly am not looking for love. I've already got that. With Bill, my husband.

Sometimes I'll say to Bill, "You're the best fuck I've ever had in my whole life." And it's the truth. I just like variety.

I've changed over the years. My first "extra" wasn't so great. He'd get an erection and then in two seconds flat it would melt away. And he didn't ejaculate. We kept trying and I kept thinking, "Maybe I can help him." But I don't go for that role now. I've given it up. No more. It's a waste of time. There are plenty of men out there who *can* make it.

Take Bill, my husband. He's incredible. He has amazing timing. He keeps an erection, waits for me, doesn't climax before I do.

Bill was my first lover. When I was eighteen. I got into bed nude and put the pillow over my head because I was too embarrassed to look at him. It was my first look at a naked man. He got into bed and said, "Come on out from under that pillow. Relax. This is going to be fun. I promise you, you'll like it." And I did, I did. I'll never forget it. It was such a nice introduction to fucking.

And guess what? He told me later that he was scared, too. It was *his* first experience. He's great. I love him dearly. I don't think he has other women. I'm enough for him.

I love my kids, too. I like being a mother, but I'm not doing the Freudian bit of being over-enchanted with my sons. They're not my life. They're a big, important part of it, but they're not the whole thing. They don't have to fulfill all my needs. Why should they? They've got lives of their own.

So now you're probably wondering, why do I do it? Why do I get involved with other men, especially when they usually end up falling in love with me, and then there's a big scene when I have to cut out?

Simple. I like sex. I need a lot of orgasms. But I'm not going to force Bill to give me more than he wants to. And like I said, I enjoy variety.

I used to worry. "I'm promiscuous," I said to myself. "What am I going to do about it?" I went to a therapist for a couple of months and we got nowhere. One day it dawned on me: so I love sex. So what? I'm a good wife, a good mother, so what's the problem? Now I don't go to anyone for advice.

Once I got involved with this young guy. I thought, "Well, he's young; he'll give me all the stuff I can handle." We were sitting on the couch at his place, and it took him fifteen minutes to put his arm around me. I said to myself, "God, it'll take *months* at this rate."

Finally I said, "Listen, let's go to bed," and he began to apologize. He said he had no experience. He'd had sex only once before. The kid was twenty-four! Can you believe it!

I told him not to worry and off we went to bed. We get there and bang, he jumps on me and comes, one-two-three and it's over. Well, it was pretty awful, but I liked the kid and I decided to teach him some of the finer points.

I taught him how to kiss. I told him what to do with his hands. I showed him how to arouse a woman slowly, gradually. I told him about the clitoris and how to stroke it lightly, sensitively, until you can feel the juices flowing. By the end of three months he could have gone anywhere as one of the great lovers of our time.

Then I got bored and I moved on. He was hurt, but he'll live. Men always get to a point where they want too much from me. Some want me to be faithful. There were two who wanted me to divorce Bill.

But, no. I'll never do that. Faithfulness is a state of mind. What you do with your body is not that important. I know where my home is. I know who the primary human being in my life is: Bill.

Believe me, if for any reason he felt threatened by my extracurricular activities, I'd stop cold. Just like that. No, we never talk about it. That game is for children. What married people do individually is their own business. This ridiculous honesty where husbands and wives tell each other about their affairs is for the birds.

All my life I've kept my mouth shut about my sexuality. Now that I'm in my thirties, I feel freer inside myself. Also, the world is freer about sex now. But I'm still inhibited when it comes to talking sex with a bunch of women. Most of them aren't like me. They wouldn't understand. I have the feeling that if I talked about it, they'd end up not trusting me. They'd all lock their husbands in the closet when I came around. But I also have this idea that it's important for women to really, you know, communicate on the subject.

I have a friend. She's thirty-three and married and, believe it or not, she's never had an orgasm. When she told me, I actually cried. I felt so bad for her. She doesn't even know what she's missing.

I'm not sure why I kept track, but in all the years

I've been having sex—seventeen years to be exact—I missed having an orgasm fifteen times. I have sharp orgasms, not multiple, not a series. I don't exactly understand that ... a "multiple" orgasm ... but I keep reading about it in the sex books.

I know a lot of women who are at the mercy of their men. They have nothing to bargain with. Just sex. And then they use sex to get things from their husbands. Sex as a weapon. Ugh. I don't know what the answer is. Maybe if they had more power in other areas ... ?

I sound like a women's libber, but I'm not. I mean I don't belong to any group. I don't like the extremists. They think that having sex with a man is the same as letting yourself be used or dominated or something. Well ... look at me. Nobody uses me. If anything, it's the other way around. I use men. Wait a minute. That's not true, either. Men and women, they ought to use each other. But in a nice way, you know? We need each other.

Until very recent efforts to strike out for more freedom, most women have been seduced—and understandably so—by the protection offered by marriage, bartering self for security.

Joyce has taken up a stance midway between freedom and security. She risks being rejected by the men she approaches for sex. But the pain of rejection, when it occurs, is somewhat softened by her knowledge that whatever happens on the outside, she has a warm, loving husband at home, along with all the social and financial advantages of being married.

Still Joyce is definitely sexually aggressive because more often than not it is she, not the male, who makes the initial approach; she, not the male, who defines the limits of each new relationship. Though she speaks with fondness of some of her lovers, she does not romanticize her affairs and is clearly able to separate love from passion. Often, her casual, non-possessive attitude elicits an opposite reaction from her lovers, who become emotionally and sexually dependent on her.

Though she's a tough, no-nonsense person with little tolerance for false sentiment, she is not a "put-down" woman, as she easily could have been with men who were timid or inexperienced. Patient and reassuring with her twenty-four-year-old virgin lover, she tells us, "By the end of three months he could have gone anywhere as one of the great lovers of our time."

Her relationship with her husband, built on state-of-mind faithfulness, is not unique among sexually aggressive wives and mothers and may be the kind toward which more and more men and women (sexually aggressive or not) are moving. Certainly "adultery" is on the rise, and if marriage as an institution is to survive at all, it may have to be with the understanding that what one does with one's body is one's own business and needn't interfere with one's feelings for one's mate.

Annette

"In marriage, you get careless, sloppy . . . you don't get that fantastic rush each time."

Annette, a thirty-three-year-old advertising agency executive, is married now for the second time. She earns good money, enjoys her job, and has decided for the time being that children are out of the question.

"Vibrant" is the word for her. She radiates energy, and it is this quality that makes her seem far more attractive than she really is. Her movements, like her speech, are quick and purposeful, although at times one detects a nervous edge in her voice.

Though she answered my ad because she wanted to talk about her sexuality, she absolutely refused to call herself "sexually aggressive"—a label she considers negative.

Sexually aggressive, to me, is the gal who goes into a bar and says, "Hey, you turn me on, let's screw." I could *never* do that. I think I'm old-fashioned, really.

But, well ... just last night my husband had to work late, so I went to the theater alone. I sat in the third row and looked at the male lead and thought, "Would I love to get that guy into bed." He was my

43

type—a cross between Jean-Paul Belmondo and Joel Grey. Lean. Sort of mean and hard like Humphrey Bogart. A hint of the bastard.

My agency handles promotion for the theater where the play was being performed, so I had a good excuse to go backstage afterwards and meet him. But ... by that time I was turned off him. He was a lousy actor. I can't stand second-rate actors. Second-rate anything.

But I would have gone after him if I'd felt like it.

My husband and I don't talk about outside sex. No discussion of our activities. I chose him because I knew we could share our lives, but at the same time I could do my own thing. Otherwise it wouldn't work. He feels the same way. We don't sit around making conversation about our other relationships. When we're together, we're really together.

But when I see a guy I like, I move in. Last month we were at a party and I met this man. He was with one of the most beautiful women I've ever seen. A model type. Incredible long blonde hair. Perfect features. I'm not that at all. But I had to have this guy this model girl was with.

I started the conversation: "You're simply the most attractive man I've ever met in my entire life." I can say things like that. Other women can't. Flattery ... it always works. But you have to know how to do it. He immediately asked me out to dinner.

I met him at the restaurant and I made sure we sat *across* from each other. I like to *look* at the guy. I began with the flirting. I'm good at that, too. I roll my eyes, do a little "accidental" touching. Within an hour he was wanting to get into my pants.

But mostly I'm more verbal than physical. I come on soulful. Poetic. I told one guy he had an absolutely Promethean body. He did. It wasn't a lie. I often throw in a little mythology. It's impressive. The guys I meet usually know enough about Greek gods, so it works.

A lot of men have said they've never met anyone who understands them the way I do. Bullshit. Most women just don't take the trouble to find the weak, vulnerable spot and play to it. I usually begin by probing for his sensitivities.

Pain. That's a good one. One night I was with a guy at the theater. We saw *The Gingerbread Man*, and we both thought it was ugly. Afterwards we went for a drink, and I began talking about all the pain we carry with us. All the time. It's a good opener. Everyone is in some kind of pain. If you can find out about the pain, you know where that person is at. But it works better after you've had a few cognacs.

Once I went to a psychiatrist. After three sessions, he said "You don't need me. You let everything out. You use your emotions and it works for you."

I do accept myself most of the time. I know I need a husband; being married gives structure to my life, and I love Gene. I do. I also need other men. It's the way I'm made.

But with other guys, it has to have a romantic, soft-lights beginning, or I don't pursue it. I could never meet somebody and say, "I'll see you at the Ritz Hotel for fucking at ten P.M." It's not in my nature.

When I'm in bed, I let things happen. But in a

planned sort of way. I never *tell* him what I want. But I get it by moving his hands. I'm big on compliments, too. I'll say, "If you were one inch shorter or I were one inch taller, we wouldn't make it together. But we're perfect."

I'm having an affair now with a young man who is fabulous. Just fabulous. We don't see each other often because we don't need to. When it's good, it's good, and the feeling carries over from one time to the next. Like last week. I'm still feeling the glow. After sex, we had dinner and wine. We don't talk about our "relationship"—incidentally, I *hate* that word—because it kind of spoils things. He said, "Honest to God, Annette, I think you're great. And I know damn well that if I were one inch shorter or you were one inch taller it wouldn't be as good. We're just perfectly physically made for each other."

He was using my line, but in this case it's true. The perfect fit.

When I fuck I make the most gorgeous fantasies about how I got the guy there because *I* wanted him there and then comes a giant orgasm that almost throws me out of the bed.

The first time with a man, when we're playing around and his fingers are off base, I'll just move his hand ever so gently to where I want it, and if he's too rough, I'll lift it and move it the way I like it.

Once in a while I meet a guy who just doesn't understand what I want. Even after I've helped him find out. This kind of guy is insensitive. He might be a fine person otherwise, but I don't want to fuck with him. Listen, the best prick in the world doesn't make up for insensitivity or a lack of enthusiasm.

I remember times when I sat on my first husband's lap and did everything to please him and he'd push me away. He was insensitive. So, within six months, I met a really nice-looking attorney. He liked to go places, do interesting things. I started going with him back and forth to San Juan and living a sort of jet-set life. There was mucho sex, so I figured I had it aced. I was still in love with my first husband—can you believe it? I had a tremendous affection for him but we didn't, you know, meet each other's needs. And I was having so much fun with Ed—the attorney. We figured, what the hell, let's get married. He left his wife and I left my husband.

But Ed and I never got married. By the time he'd left his wife and I was in the process of divorcing my husband, I'd fallen in love with Gene, my present husband. He was totally different from the other two. A peaceful, serene, accepting kind of guy.

I haven't said much about Gene. He's a good fucker. Underneath that calm exterior is a ton of enthusiasm. With him, I come one hundred percent of the time.

With a lover, when I don't come, I get a little pissy and cool. I get up. I start to pace around. Look through a magazine. But I don't say, "You son of a bitch, you left me hanging! What are you going to do about it?" That's my idea of bad form.

If you want to get analytical about it, I guess there's no such thing as taking turns with orgasms. It happens or it doesn't. It's my responsibility to see that I get mine. I let the guy know how and where and how long to play with my clitoris and my nipples. If it doesn't work, I guess I can't really blame it on him.

Frankly, I prefer the good old-fashioned missionary position. I hate being on top because I'm physically clumsy. Poorly coordinated. I got thrown out of dancing school, flunked gym. Being on top is hard work anyway. . . .

So either I lie back, or else I go down on all fours, or sometimes I lean against the bed and he comes up behind me. That's fun sometimes.

Anal sex . . . it makes me want to puke just to think about it.

One summer I went off to Europe with the idea of experimenting. I'd just broken up with a guy and I was—don't laugh, now—I was heartbroken. In Portugal I met another guy. I liked him fine, but he had a lot of friends and they all made it together. I tried doing the group thing with them and I didn't like it. I loved watching, though.

My husband and I have an agreement. We go away once a year together, and then we each take another separate vacation. We both come back refreshed.

I think I like the glamour and excitement and romance of sex as much as I enjoy sex itself. On my last separate vacation, I went to the Caribbean. One night I was having a cocktail alone on a terrace overlooking the sea. I saw a man, the Belmondo type I always go for, and I stared at him. I enveloped him with my eyes. Just sitting there, I directed all my energy toward him.

It worked. He stared back. In fifteen minutes we were sharing a table, laughing, getting acquainted.

It wouldn't have happened if I was with a girlfriend. Two women can't play that game.

Anyway, we went riding off in his car—far up into the mountains where you can still smell the sea, feel the wind. The sun was setting. Total glamour and romance. I like that. I like high living. Good wine. Elegant food.

Clothes? I hate anything that's obviously sexy. No clingy dresses. No see-through stuff. The kind of man I like would think those things are tacky. Mostly I wear pants or skirts with sweaters and little tank tops.

I'm financially independent. My husband and I pool our funds but I could live nicely on my own. Still, when I'm out with a guy—my husband or anybody else—I want him to pay the bills.

That's the way I am. I want to be underwritten. But that doesn't make me feel beholden. It's a fair trade. I go someplace with a man and he pays for the pleasure of my company.

Next week I'm going off on a trip, with my *mother*. And my current boyfriend is picking up the tab. My husband was married once before, so he's spending that week with his children. My boyfriend is busy but he wants me to enjoy myself. What's the big deal?

My mother is old now, in her seventies, and she needs some fun. She knows the score. She's aware of my activities. She was poor. She worked hard all her life. She tells me to get the most from every moment, to grab everything I can get. I can be honest with her.

But not with my husband. Honesty is a good

thing, but carried past a certain point it can be destructive. I would never hurt anyone in the name of honesty.

Lovers on the side are a sexual bonus. In marriage, you get careless, sloppy. You don't get that fantastic rush each time, because you know this nice, wonderful guy is still going to be there next week, and the week after that. Having lovers keeps you on your toes. It makes sex with your husband even nicer. It does for me, anyway.

I don't know why I'm the way I am. When I was sixteen, my grandmother saw me kissing a boy on the front steps and she screamed at me, "You're a whore. A bad girl." She came from Poland and maybe by her standards that's what I was.

I understand her point of view, but it came from another place and time. Now I say "Screw society." I feel together, I have a good job, I love my husband. Life is beautiful. Even the painful parts.

No woman has to be alone in a room crying her eyes out about a man that's gone. "Get out and fuck someone else"—that's my advice. When you meet someone, focus on him. *Feel* you're irresistible, and you will be. Last year I took a mind control course and they didn't tell me anything I didn't already know. Focus and no one can resist you; no one can ever resist being the center of someone else's universe. That's how I operate and that's why I'm good with men.

Anyway, that's one of my few rules. Mostly I ignore the rest. You're better off if you do. What do rules have to do with the lives we live today? Even my grandmother would feel differently if she were living now.

A fascinating element of doublethink runs through Annette's story. She does one thing and calls it another because she cannot quite accept her behavior for what it is. She plays semantic tricks with the term "sexually aggressive woman," deciding it applies mainly to "the gal who goes into a bar and says, 'Hey, you turn me on, let's screw.'" Certainly, she is not that kind of woman. So, by limiting the definition, she can justify her actions and even call herself "old-fashioned."

True, she makes use of some very "old-fashioned" tricks indeed. She is not above rolling her eyes, using flowery verbal flattery, noting individual male sensitivities, and basing her strategies for seduction on them. That she considers it right and proper for her men to foot the bills might also be considered "old-fashioned" by some few women, although the custom is still taken for granted by most.

But she is totally contemporary in her insistence on a variety of sexual partners and her desire to experiment. She is in no way hampered by the fact that she cares for her husband; but she does feel some anxiety lest he discover the extent of her activities. She initiates extramarital affairs and controls the sexual episodes themselves by indicating how the man can bring her to orgasm. Thus, she is sexually aggressive, no matter how she tries to squirm free of the definition.

Of special interest, I think, is the attitude of Annette's aged mother. Extrapolating from her own ex-

perience, the mother sees that a life of toil and self-sacrifice brings no special earthly rewards, and she urges Annette to get the most from every minute, to grab everything she can get, hoping that her daughter's life will be richer than her own ever could have been.

Cindy

"I decided I had to have an affair, just to prove I could do it."

Cindy is one of those petite, gamin-faced young women who manage to look twelve until they're in their forties. In reality, she is twenty-three.

She sits forward on the edge of her chair, and speaks in a soft, child-like voice. She seems very anxious to please.

Her marriage is five years old and so is her child. She lives in a neat little attached house in a lower-middle-class section of a big Eastern city. One gets the feeling on entering that house that money is a problem for the people who live there.

Me? I'm *sort* of sexually aggressive. I mean, with my husband. I've had one affair, but otherwise, I'm faithful. "Sexually aggressive" makes me think of a woman who is more free-spirited than I am, who sleeps with lots and lots of men.

Most of my friends are single and they call me up every morning to tell me who they slept with the night before. I think they're just out to please themselves. Sometimes I'd like to do the same. Sometimes I think it's silly to be married.

But I'm old-fashioned. I was pregnant when I got

married. Bob was my first love. I was very passive with him. And dumb. I let him do whatever he wanted. Birth control ... it never entered my mind. I could have had an abortion. When my parents found out I was pregnant they sent me to a psychiatrist. Right away, in that first hour, I knew I wanted to have the baby. It was part of me and Bob. Bob felt the same way.

Sometimes I envy my single friends. They're having fun. I missed that kind of fun. But marriage is right for me. Loving someone makes me feel good. Being loved gives me security. . . .

The very first time I went to bed with Bob I loved it. I also felt guilty. I knew my parents would feel just awful if they found out. But I didn't let it stop me. I was sixteen then, and all my friends were either very prudish or very free. One of my girlfriends kept saying, "Go all the way with Bob. Why not? After a while it doesn't make sense to hold out any longer. You're his steady." I kept thinking, "Should I, or shouldn't I?"

I had orgasms with him even before we had real sex. Bob masturbated me. I did it to him, too. Even now he masturbates me twice, anyway, before intercourse. He usually has just one orgasm.

I always remember Rod Steiger's line about "How can someone get married on the way to their first orgasm?" I love it.

Anyway, when I got pregnant at eighteen, we got married and now we're just an average couple. Our sex life was average, too. He'd come after me more than I went after him. *Sometimes* I was the aggressor, but it wasn't because I felt like it. It was more of an ego trip.

Then one morning after he left for work, I thought to myself, "I bet he'd really get turned on if I changed things." I don't know why I thought about it. Maybe it wasn't very exciting the night before.

It used to happen this way: we'd be sitting watching TV, and after a while he'd move in closer, a kind of sly grin on his face, and then I'd know where his head was at. He'd kiss me on the neck, we'd undress each other, we'd get into bed and do it. We used to have sex on certain days—not Monday, Wednesday, and Saturday. Not like that. But every third day. It got to be a routine.

Anyway, I decided to try something different. When he came home that night I was in the kitchen, and I just stood there with my hands on my hips and said, "Hey, do you want to fuck?" He just looked at me like I was crazy and then he said, "I can't believe you said that." I had *never* used that word before.

That was the beginning. The next time I really attacked him. I jumped on him and started biting his neck, acting silly. It was fun for me, but not sexy, or sensual. But then when I saw how it turned *him* on, I got very passionate.

I make sure of one thing. *I* decide when I am going to be the aggressor. Sometimes, I will, but not all the time. And not always in the same way.

Another reason why I got into this new kick was because my friends kept saying how sorry they were for me that I had only one man. Rubbing it in. Not in a vicious way, but still ...

My friends egg me on. They work in offices and they're into women's lib, some of them, and they say *why* is the woman supposed to wash the dishes? Or, why is she supposed to wait for the man to call and ask for a date? They tell me how after work when they see a groovy guy on the street, they walk right up and start a conversation, simply because they like the way he looks.

Well, I love sex with Bob. I never felt horny or hung up or unfulfilled or anything like that, but I kept thinking about my friends and what they do.

I decided I *had* to have an affair just to prove I could do it. I wanted to see what it would be like. So one night when Bob was out bowling, I went out with a girlfriend. We went to a bar, I saw a nice-looking guy—not spectacular, just nice—and I started talking to him. Finally I came right out with it: "I want you. Let's fuck." It was okay, but not as good as with Bob. After a few times with that guy, I decided to cut it out. It was never any big deal. I'd proved my point—that I could get a strange man into bed with me if I wanted to—and I guess that was the important thing. Now I don't sleep with anyone but Bob.

Sometimes, when I'm really turned on, I'll start fantasizing before he comes home from work. I even play with my own nipples. My breasts are my most sensitive area. Sometimes I come all by myself, just touching my own breasts.

Anyway, when I'm in the mood for some really heavy sex, I'll see that Bobby, Jr., is in bed early. Then when Bob comes in I grab him, touch his balls, and lead him into the bedroom.

Once we're in bed, I plunge right for his penis and suck him, although we don't always do 69. I don't like it when we're sucking each other at the same time. But I love it when he sucks me or I suck him. I can keep doing it forever, but I always stop if I think he's going to come right away.

Then I ask him to play with my breasts and suck my nipples, because they're so super sensitive. I think I said that before. They're more sensitive than my clitoris.

I like to be on top during intercourse because the angle of his penis really sets up a lot of friction on my clitoris. I like dog-style, too, with me on the bottom and him on the top, his stomach to my back; I rest my head on a pillow and both my hands are free and I can do anything I want with them. Another one that's good for a really big charge is when I lie on my stomach, but flat to the bed, and he's on top with his stomach to my back. That way, my clitoris rubs against the sheets and it's fantastic.

There's only one thing I won't do and that is letting him put his penis in my rectum ... anal sex. He wants to sometimes, but I always tell him no. I swear, sometimes he seems relieved about it. He reads all the sex books and they make you feel you're not getting the most out of sex unless you've tried *everything*. Well, I won't do it just because some book says I should.

The change in my sexual behavior is good for both of us. My friends say I was a victim of male chauvinism, and I know now that they were right—at least there were times when I used to give in, even when I didn't want to. Now I'm the one who says when, and I'm the one who says how. He's never, never turned me down. Sometimes I wish he would reject me. Not often, but once in a while. That would prove I really *am* aggressive.

Cindy, in a minor way, is rebelling against male chauvinism. Obviously strongly influenced by her unmarried, more sexually aggressive friends, she has decided she needn't acquiesce to her man. She refuses anal sex. She initiates intercourse. She deliberately set out to have an affair, handled it without guilt, and, just as important, was able to end it when it no longer pleased her. And so, she is a sexually aggressive woman, although she stays well within careful, self-imposed limits. She sees her new assertiveness mostly as a way to liven up her relationship with Bob. (A more aggressive woman would view it as an enhancement of her own pleasure.) I'd be willing to bet that twenty-five years ago, a woman like Cindy would have accepted without question the role of passive, selfless wife and mother assigned her by the culture of that time.

Isabel

"I'm going out there to find a woman to sleep with my husband."

Isabel, at forty-five, is a big, striking-looking woman with salt-and-pepper hair, large, nicely-shaped features, and what used to be called "good carriage." She walks, stands, and sits straight and tall.

For several years now, she has managed a small boutique on the West Coast. She and her husband Leonard—who is a doctor and fifteen years her senior—have been married (happily, she insists) for twenty-three years. Their two children are now in college.

Isabel is another woman who can't quite decide whether she fits the sexually aggressive category.

But she was eager to tell her story.

I love Leonard dearly. It hurts me to see how depressed he's become in the past year. He can hardly drag himself out of bed in the morning. I have a feeling he's taking amphetamines to get him through the day. As a doctor, he can get as much as he wants and it scares me.

It seems he's beginning to look at himself as an old man. He tells me he's crossed that invisible line between middle age and old age. He has no interest in sex. I don't know much about these things, but it seems that sixty is too young to give it up.

His family was very religious, and he's followed their beliefs. To have an affair ... even to look at another woman ... I don't think he's ever allowed himself to do it. I'd stake my life on it.

Our sex was once very good. I suppose you could say we "aggressed" each other. I asked for orgasms and I got orgasms.

I had an affair once. I did it out of curiosity, pure and simple. But I came running back to Leonard.

I've felt very secure in our marriage. It's the security that made it possible for me to raise two children, run the shop, and ... just thoroughly enjoy my life. I always knew Leonard was with me one hundred percent.

He's still with me. In his mind, in his heart, in his soul. But he's impotent. I can't arouse him. He rolls away from me in bed. I hold him, touch him, do everything I know how to do to awaken his interest, and he doesn't even get an erection.

But I feel it's just me. Twenty-three years of sex with the same person ... it's got to be boring. How can it be anything else? All those books and magazine articles that tell you how to rejuvenate your sex life! Go to a motel! Wear seductive lingerie! Dye your hair! I ... we've ... tried it all.

At night I see him lying there, staring into space.

Well, what else can you expect? When you've been with one body for so long and you've seen that body on the toilet, or sick in bed with the flu, and you know every single freckle and mole, and you know precisely how it'll react to anything you do, sex just loses something. It has to. I'm not complaining. Sometimes I cry, but I do accept it.

Poor Leonard. He can't accept it. He can't admit that sex is part of his problem. He'd feel disloyal if he admitted even to himself that I don't excite him. And even if he did admit it, he'd never do anything about it. Never go out to find himself another woman. Instead, he'd sit and wither away, and my real fear is he'll die of it.

Maybe they'll call it a heart attack or stroke, but I truly believe that people die when they're ready. When there's no more joy, they die—because there's nothing to live for.

And, so, finally, I'll come to the point. I feel in my heart that one thing—and one thing only—will bring him back to life: another woman. A fresh body, with different odors, hands, hair, breasts ... a brand-new experience.

She shouldn't be too young. A twenty-year-old would remind him of our daughter, Sally. He could never sleep with anyone like that. But an attractive woman in her late thirties ... a little younger than me. That kind of woman would be exactly right.

I know it. I just feel it in my heart. And that's why I think I'm a sexually aggressive woman in some oddball way. Because I'm going out there to find a woman to sleep with my husband!

I don't love the idea. It fills me with conflict. It certainly doesn't fit in with anything I believe in. But a man's life is at stake. A man I love deeply.

And, honestly, I know as well as any woman can know these things that even if Leonard was turned on sexually, he would never leave me. We've been through too much together—the kids, getting his career started, our friends—everything.

So . . . I found a really expensive call girl through a friend of mine. My friend is in politics. Politicians always seem to know women like that. I told this call girl all about Leonard, and his impotence, and then I sent her to him as a patient. Now the rest is up to her.

I'm sure that over the years some women have tried to make him. But when he's looking up your nose or down your throat or into your ears—he's a nose and throat specialist, you know—it's not exactly conducive to sex, romance . . . whatever you want to call it. But a really experienced woman, a call girl—she'd have tricks I never even thought of.

I have a few that used to work. Like rubbing up against him when he's dressed. Just lightly holding him against a wall. Running my finger over his lips. Taking out his penis when we're in the living room. (Saving sex for the bedroom—that's dull.) Anyway, maybe some of my old tricks will work again, after the call girl has had a chance at him.

I had another idea, but I gave it up. I thought of bringing in a second woman, so it would be a trio: Leonard and me and some fresh new body. But knowing Leonard, he'd be very polite and offer to make lunch and divert the whole thing into a proper little social gathering.

I suppose a lot of people would never, never understand why I'm doing this. But I love him and I want him—alive and happy. Am I sexually aggressive?

I found Isabel a most remarkable woman. Thoroughly conventional by all outward appearances, she enjoys sex and has always been relatively assertive in her own bed with her own husband. The imaginative and seemingly selfless ploy of selecting a call girl for her husband is not, on second consideration so very selfless, after all: if her strategy works and Leonard regains an interest in sex, Isabel, too, stands to gain by it. I doubt that many forty-five-year-old women would even conceive such a plan. Far fewer would act on it.

As a sexually aggressive woman—and, yes, I would say she does qualify as one—Isabel is selfless, selfish, caring, and—unique.

Chapter 3

THE WOMAN ALONE

To this very considerable portion of female humanity [unmarried women], the right to the exercise and enjoyment of their sexual instincts is absolutely denied, under penalty of social death.

VICTORIA WOODHULL (1874)

The times they *are* achanging, but for many unmarried women they haven't changed all *that* much. A woman is still assumed to be better off when she is being taken care of by a man. And though society as a whole has, finally, acknowledged the right of the woman alone to make what she wants of her life—up to a point—there are still those for whom it comes as a bit of a shock to learn that an unmarried woman is sexually active. Celibacy, with all its attendant frustrations—and no matter how physically and emotionally debilitating—is more seemly.

Unfortunately, great numbers of divorced, separated, and widowed women still hold the same Victorian view and suffer enormously because of it. And so I was particularly gratified when so many of the women who contacted me in response to my ads in search of sexually aggressive women turned out to be thirty-, forty-, and fifty-year-old representatives of this group.

Most of these women have come a long, long way. The older ones were reared at a time when the pros and cons of premarital sex were not even debated. A "nice" girl was a virgin at marriage. Period. Even the younger ones were instructed that "playing hard to get" was by far the best tactic when it came to snaring a man. And snaring a man was a must. To be alone was the one fate worse than death.

Now, some of these women are discovering that aloneness can be its own reward—that while the circumstances that brought them to it were almost always painful, being on their own forced them, suddenly, into a sink-or-swim situation. And in learning to swim—to function independently—their real identities emerged.

It was not easy for any of these women. Most of them contemplated their new lives with a mixture of fear and curiosity. Especially fear. How would they get by financially? Emotionally? Sexually? How to proceed? There was bewilderment. Many had been handed over directly from their parents' homes into the care of their husbands and felt, at the age of thirty, or forty, or fifty, like orphans or adolescents newly let loose in the world. Young people can rely on their peers for comfort and guidance, but these women knew few, if any, others who were embarking on the same journey.

To have attempted the journey at all, I think, is a tribute to their courage, their strength, and their resiliency. It is one thing to be aware of new feelings and desires (and let me note that many of these women felt little or no interest in sex until they found themselves alone in the world), it's quite another to *act* upon them. The fear of embarrassment, failure, and rejection runs deep and strong.

The way people experience rejection, especially, is related to the way they've been socialized early in life. When one has grown up without the expectation of achieving through one's own efforts—as many women have grown up—then failure and rejection may come across as deserved punishment for merely trying. In which case, why try? And when one is encouraged early on simply to *be*, rather than *do*—as many women are—then failure and rejection are easily interpreted as indications of personal worthlessness. It's difficult to imagine a more painful self-judgment.

But each of these women made her own way as best she could, and it is possible to detect in all of them the exhilaration of having proved something enormously valuable to herself and about herself, the triumph of having "come through."

Some of their stories may seem tame by comparison to the tales told by other women in this book. There is a tendency, especially among the older women, to confuse sexual aggression with what many younger women might define as sexual equality. But let's not forget the point from which the older women started. One of the fifty-year-olds told me, "I was married so long ... my entire education about sex and men began just two years ago." Another woman said, "At forty-seven, I was reborn."

Many, especially the ones whose marital experiences were particularly painful, wonder whether they will ever again have a pleasurable and sound relationship with a man, based on mutual give and take. But—and this is the important point—having achieved self-sufficiency, having verified themselves as separate, worthwhile persons by living alone, by making their own way in the world, and, yes, by learning to express their sexuality, it is doubtful that any of them will ever settle for less in the long run.

Estelle

"Don't let anyone tell you it's all over for a fifty-year-old."

Estelle is fifty. Her hair, flecked here and there with silver, is done up in a sleek French twist. Her clothes are expensive: brown suede pants suit, white cashmere sweater, and what appear to be Gucci shoes. She has a fine size-ten figure, not girlish—but then she is not a girl—but "womanly" in the best sense of the word.

Her manner is gentle, ladylike, almost diffident. It's obvious to me that she is having second thoughs about the interview, and I wonder if she will offer some excuse, apologize, and leave. But she doesn't.

Her husband died two years ago. Until then she had been "just a wife and mother" (her three children are in college). She has just taken a job—her first—as secretary to a lawyer. She says she had been faithful to her husband throughout their marriage.

Yes, I am sexually aggressive. But I hate admitting it. It sounds so ... predatory. I don't like to think of myself that way.

My definition of a sexually aggressive woman? I only know what *I* do. At a party, for example, I'll walk over to an interesting-looking man and start a conversation. Inside, I feel very cold and calculating. Very objective. But I'm warm on the outside.

Of course, I'm still learning. I used to stand in a corner and wait for someone to come over and talk to me. That's no good. Maybe a sexy twenty-two-year-old can do that. But I have to come on stronger.

Anyway, I smile a lot at a party. When I walk in, I pretend I'm on stage. I have a drink, I look the situation over. I say to myself again and again, "I'm as good as anyone here." Self-hypnosis, almost. But . . . I need one tiny thing to happen before I can be aggressive. . . .

It's non-verbal. It's a certain kind of look that has to pass between me and a man. When I get this look, I just feel I am . . . I could be . . . his type. It gives me strength. Without it, I feel the next step might not work.

When I get that look, I move in. I walk over and start to talk. I talk and I listen with my eyes. Men over forty-five need eye treatment. The eyes have to radiate warmth and tenderness. They need verbal feeding too. These men are tired.

Sometimes, while we're talking, I'll shift my hip slightly. Or brush an imaginary hair off his jacket. Even "accidentally" bump his elbow—gently. Just enough to make body contact.

Maybe I'm old-fashioned but I think good listening can be terribly aggressive. I use my body when I listen. Lean way forward. Focus in close. It doesn't matter what you talk about—Nixon, soap, anything. The focus is the thing.

If I'm interested, and he doesn't ask for my number, then I ask for his. I always say something about how much I enjoyed talking to him and that I'd like to talk more. But they know what I mean. They get the message.

I was married so long! [Twenty-seven years.] I knew very little about men until two years ago when my husband died. I'm educating myself and I'm doing it now for *me*. My children are off on their own. My life and my time are mine—nobody else's. If I don't make some kind of life for myself, no one else will. It's all very obvious. Passive ladies just sit around.

Yes, I'm traditional enough to want to get married again. And the more aggressive I become, the surer I am that I can do it. But I've got to have some fun first. Play.

At first, when my husband died, I thought that was the end of it—sex, I mean. I worried that I wouldn't be able to find men. The right sort. The right age. I thought all the attractive men only wanted young girls. But it isn't so. Some of them may fantasize about younger women, but a lot of them are frightened that they won't be able to meet their sexual demands. Some of them have the feeling that they're doing something incestuous if they have a daughter the same age as the girlfriend. Anyway, there are men around who're interested in me. Don't let anyone tell you that it's all over for a fifty-year-old!

By the way, my mother is seventy-four and she has a boyfriend. He's her age. I don't know what they do in bed, but they're doing *something*, that's for certain.

The first aggressive thing I did was last year,

when I flew to Houston to visit my son at college. It was a short flight. As we went through the security check-in, I saw a man who appealed to me. He was fifty-ish. Graying hair. A nice build. Well dressed. I fussed around in my purse for a while, pretending I couldn't find something, and followed him on board. Then I sat down next to him.

Sitting down next to him was the first step. "But *now* what do I do?" I thought to myself. Well, I've always been nervous about flying, so I decided to start from there. I turned to him and said, "This is my tenth or maybe my twentieth flight, but it still scares me." Then he began to reassure me.

By the time we landed in Houston, I knew he was in an old, bad marriage, had a very demanding job, and ... he was lonely. That's another thing I've discovered. Everyone is lonely.

We had a cocktail; then my new friend suggested I visit him in his motel room later on, after I'd spent some time with my son.

As he unlocked the door of the motel room, I thought I'd vomit. This was the moment of truth. This would be my first sex in a year—and the first sex *ever* with anyone but my husband. I felt sick.

The whole business ran against every single thing I'd ever learned. "I'm fifty years old," I thought. "I'm not a kid. What am I doing here?"

Then I had another thought. "I *am* here. Because I wanted to be. I'm human. I have needs and desires. If I want any kind of life at all, I'd better start learning how to play this game."

So I sat down on the edge of the bed. I was dreadfully self-conscious. We had a drink, talked for a while about nothing, then he went into the bathroom. When he came out he was wearing his shorts. I could see his penis, bulging and erect under the shorts.

I took a deep breath, looked straight at him and said, "I'm a good talker, but the rest is up to you."

He laughed, knelt beside the bed and unbuttoned my blouse. Then he unzipped my skirt and pulled it down. I lay there in my bra and pantyhose.

He turned me toward him and started touching me, very gently. My arms, my stomach, my thighs. I began to feel less tense. I touched him, too. I kissed his ears, rubbed my lips over his stomach.

He whispered, "Do whatever you like," and that made me feel even more at ease. I stroked his penis. Held his balls in my hand. I felt good . . . strange, too. I put my mouth over his penis and began to suck. I'd done this occasionally with my husband but I always resented it—probably because he *always* asked for it.

Then he said, "You're going to be sore as hell in the morning because I've got the biggest prick . . ."

I sat up and looked at his penis. Where the next words came from I'll never know. It didn't sound like the old me. "It looks okay," I said, "but it doesn't seem any bigger than my husband's, and that's the only one I ever knew until now. I was never sore with him."

He seemed relieved, so I knew I'd chosen the right words.

My husband used to ask me to have anal sex. I always told him I couldn't do it. It seemed unnatural. But he kept on asking. About three times a year, with a couple of drinks inside him, he'd start in again. I've always hated being pushed into doing anything.

But I was curious. Now, I thought, "*I'll* ask for it." I did. I went to my purse, took out some lotion, asked him to lubricate me and turned over on my stomach.

Even the feel of the lotion was great. It was an incredible experience.

For me, sex has always been tied in with home and family and security. And although I'd refused my husband at times, it made me feel guilty. I thought I had no right to turn him down. It was my duty to have sex on demand.

But this experience made me feel very powerful. I liked that feeling. I'd asked for something and I'd got it. I wasn't being told what to do. I was doing the telling.

I stayed in Houston an extra day. We spent almost all our time in bed. I felt alive, good. I didn't feel possessive and it never crossed my mind that I was in love. I knew it would soon end and we'd go our separate ways and there was something—I guess "liberating" would be a good word for it—there was something liberating about knowing we'd say good-bye and probably never meet again.

Just before I left, we had sex just one more time. It was awful. He climbed right on top of me. No kissing, no touching, nothing. He came immediately.

I was hurt and angry. I wanted to say, "Hey, what about *me?*" But I let it go and rolled over. That was my old self at work.

But I even learned something from that. I could

let it go. Or I could ask for it. Either way, it was something I had a say about.

I discovered more about my body and my feelings in those two days than I had in years and years of marriage. Most of all, I discovered that the rest of my life is up to me.

Estelle, like almost all women of her generation, was raised to be a good wife and mother. She felt it was her "duty" (her own word) to do what her husband told her—sexually and probably in other ways as well. It's likely that her approach to motherhood was also "dutiful" and "selfless."

The pity of it all, of course, is that it took the death of her husband to shake Estelle into the realization that she has a self, along with legitimate needs and rights of her own (including the right to say no), in and out of bed.

Having been a one-man woman all her life, it's easy to imagine the blend of fear and curiosity she felt on entering a motel room with a strange man. But once there, she moved easily on to the next step: after years of resisting anal sex with her husband, she decided to initiate the act herself. At that moment, Estelle blossomed into full-fledged aggressiveness. For the first time, she was aware of her own power.

Estelle's mother, who took a lover at the age of seventy-four, was undoubtedly influential in Estelle's becoming a sexually aggressive woman. This elderly lady set a rather wonderful example for her daughter, who may in turn serve as a model for other women who find themselves alone in their middle years.

Betsey

"If a man doesn't like my honest approach, he probably wouldn't be very good in bed."

Betsey, forty-one, is short and slightly overweight. Her face is lovely—skin the texture of fine porcelain, eyes a misty gray-green and enormous.

She is a quiet, deliberate person, and she told her story as if she had given it quite a bit of thought.

Twice married, recently divorced for the second time, Betsey now earns her living as an advertising copywriter. She lives with her five-year-old daughter.

I left my second husband just a few months ago. I married him because I decided I wanted a baby, but I didn't want to be an unwed mother.

I married the first time when I was eighteen. I was an only child, and, quite frankly, I was anxious to get out of the house. My mother and father were delighted to see me settled. What a joke!

I was just out of high school and we were like two children playing house, trying to behave like grownups. He was going to college and I worked to send him through.

For a while it was fun, but soon I began to resent working at jobs I hated so that *he* could get his degree. I began to think, "Hey, what about *me?*" I worked, worked, worked all day, and when I came home I did the shopping, the cooking, the cleaning. We never went out; he was too busy studying. It was a horrible life. He was getting everything and I got nothing. Maybe that's why I began to focus on sex. It was the only fun I had.

At first he was terrified of sex. He was a very straight, hungup person. When we married, he was only twenty, and he'd grown up with the idea that you couldn't sleep with a "nice girl"—like me, I suppose—until you married her.

I helped him loosen up. The longer I was married, the more I liked sex. I found some serious sex books—there weren't many popular paperbacks on the market back then—and proceeded to study the subject. You might say I became an amateur sexologist.

I learned about all the erogenous zones, their proper names, the specific ways in which a woman and man are aroused.

I remember lying on the bed with a mirror between my legs so that I could see the different parts—the clitoris, the labia, the whole vaginal area. Once you pull the pubic hair back, there's a whole other world down there, and most women don't even know what it looks like.

I used to love talking sex with my husband. I used clinical words—the one from the books—and "dirty" words. He was embarrassed at first, but it always turned him on. He never had problems getting an erection.

In time, I got him to the point where he really enjoyed screwing. He even liked licking and kissing my asshole. What went wrong with our marriage really had very little to do with sex. Boredom, I think, was the problem. And the feeling that life was passing me by.

At twenty-five, I'd been married for *eight years*. I'd gone straight from my parents' house to my husband's house and in my whole life nothing very interesting had happened. All I had to look forward to was more of the same. I remember thinking to myself how sad it would be to be an old woman and have nothing to think back about. No wonderful memories. Just this blah, dull life.

Luckily, we had no children. We were both brought up Catholic, but somehow I had the good sense to go out and get myself a diaphragm. Where I got this independent notion, how I was able to perceive that my life would become one huge horror and I'd be stuck forever in this blah situation if I didn't take it in hand myself, I'll never know. But I used the diaphragm and I didn't get pregnant, and, at twenty-six, when my husband was finished with school, I left him.

He was bewildered. He didn't understand why I had to do it—and that was part of our problem; from his point of view things were just ducky.

I found a furnished room, got one of those "jobs-with-a-future" in an ad agency, and was out on my own for the first time. The feeling of freedom was marvelous. Coming and going whenever *I* wanted to, eating and sleeping when *I* felt like it. Marvelous. Just marvelous!

As for sex, I decided I'd get that, too, my own

way. I was cultivating a whole new approach to life, a free and honest one, and I saw no reason not to be consistent.

At a party, if I met someone I liked, I'd tell him outright, "I don't feel like being alone tonight. Will you come home with me?"

Of course I've been turned down. But I feel this way: if a man doesn't like my honest approach, he probably wouldn't be very good in bed.

I like to sit up on a man—preferably a big man. I have more control and I can move better when I'm on top. It's important for me to be able to look at him, to see the excitement on his face. That adds to my pleasure. I never met a man who didn't like being under me. I don't understand why so many people prefer the other way.

Here's one of my routines: I tell the man to stand still in the middle of the room, and then I undress him. Strip him down. Then I leave him standing there nude for a few minutes while I just look. I take my time. Then I walk over, kneel down and suck him until he gets an erection. It turns me on just to think of it. Then I move away again and watch him while I get undressed. I usually have some music going, and often I do a slow, sexy dance as I come back to him.

I sway back and forth for a while, brushing against him very lightly. Then I pull away. Then down we go to the floor ... well, really it's a heavy, beautiful, Oriental rug.

Sometimes I wet my lips when I suck him, and then kiss him on the mouth so that he has the taste of himself on his own lips. Maybe he does the same to me. I love tasting me through a man's kisses after he's sucked me.

Most of what I do in bed, it just happens. Except that I always show a man how to manipulate my clitoris. I take his finger and place it exactly on the tip . . . right there.

If I feel after all the foreplay that I'm not going to make it—have an orgasm when he puts his penis in— then I'll have him play with my clitoris at the same time. It's fantastic that way. Or, when one orgasm isn't enough and I want another one and he either can't get it up or doesn't want to, I simply ask him to manipulate my clitoris. Strange. That kind of orgasm is still more powerful than the so-called vaginal kind.

I wish, oh, how I wish I could be as aggressive at the office, in my work. I'm good at my job, but I'd be even better if I could operate a little more authoritatively. I got this particular job by seducing the boss—a very old-fashioned, female thing to do, but there was a reason: he couldn't decide whether to hire me or someone else. He said we were equally qualified. So I made up his mind for him by sleeping with him.

I still go to church occasionally. I love the pageantry and I believe in prayer. I really do. But I don't go to confession any more. The last time I did, I told the priest I was sexually active. He seemed very disturbed by what I said, and I thought to myself, "It's not nice of me to tell this old man such things. He's upset." So I went outside and said three Hail Marys and three Our Fathers and prayed that he'd soon get over any distress I'd caused him.

My second husband was a stud. Tall. Good-looking. Healthy. Intelligent. I chose him because I thought that together we could make a marvelous child. We agreed before we got married that I would have other sex partners when I wanted them. I assured him that I considered him free to do whatever he wanted, too.

Marriage number two didn't break up over sex either. When I hear about couples getting divorced because of sexual incompatibility, I want to laugh. It seems very silly. Each person is capable of such a wide range of feeling, and there are so many different ways to relate to any human being, that to be totally involved sexually, or any other way, with one person is ridiculous.

Anyway, I soon discovered that my second husband didn't want to work. He was a sociologist when we met. He had a good research job. I got pregnant almost immediately and then ... out of nowhere, he tells me he wants to go and live in the country. "On what?" I asked him. He thought *I* would be capable of supporting our little family. Well, I suppose I could have done it, but I didn't want to. We stayed together until Diane, our daughter, was born, and then he went off to live on some communal farm.

A good friend, a woman, moved in with me and we shared expenses. I stayed home for a year to care for Diane, then I hired a sitter and went back to work.

Diane is a beautiful, happy child and whatever she wants to know I tell her, although I always take her level of understanding into consideration. Someone was here the other night, for example. Diane woke up and told me she heard some noises. I explained to her that what she heard was two people making love, that when people make love they sometimes make noise.

Sometimes I think I have Don Juanism. But that's okay with me. A few years ago, I went to a male psychiatrist. Diane was a baby; I was a little confused. I thought maybe I should settle down, live right. Whatever *that* means. The shrink told me my pattern was "sick," that I was the aggressor and that had something to do with my getting involved with dependent men. According to him, my way of life was all wrong.

I thought about it—ten sessions' worth—and decided I didn't *feel* sick at all. A little confused, maybe, but basically okay. I like making my own decisions. I like living the way I live. I know lots of people who live differently and they're not happy either. So how am I wrong? It has always seemed to me that psychiatry ought to help people come to terms with themselves, and I've already done that.

I'm not complicated. I have no big fantasies about anything. I wanted independence and I have it. I wanted a child and I have one. I wanted to live freely and honesly and I do.

I expect honesty in return. Dishonesty is very upsetting. Like when a man pretends to be in love and he isn't. Pretending isn't necessary.

Last year I met a Frenchman. Right away he came on with a line about how "enchanted" he was with me, how he was "falling in love" with me on the spot. He practically swooned at my feet.

I don't usually speak so bluntly, but I couldn't help myself. "Cut the crap," I said. "If you want to screw, come on up to my place."

We went. His capacity was memorable—four fucks in four hours. It was a marvelous experience, but all the while he kept saying, "I love you, I love you." Absurd! How could he possibly expect me to believe it? He was insulting my intelligence.

He spent the night. Before he went to sleep, he turned off my alarm clock. I woke up at nine-thirty, and I should have been at the office at that time.

I was furious. "How *dare* you?" I screamed. He said he was only thinking of me; he said I was tired, I should rest, relax. What he really wanted was for me to skip work and fuck some more.

Lack of honesty—that seems to be the basic problem. The social scientists are just beginning to admit that women probably need more sex than men but society has always pretended it was the other way around. And then they wonder why women are so crazy and mixed up!

At forty-one, I feel just about ready for a lasting relationship. It took me this long to know myself. Even if I found a good person, though, I would never, ever promise to be sexually faithful. I won't deliberately go out and look for someone else to fuck. But if I meet an attractive man and the time and the place are right . . .

My father was a loving man. In his later years we became *very* close. He knew about my two divorces, of course, but I never told him the details of my life. I never wanted to hurt him. But he must have known. He said something amazing in the hospital just a few days before he died. "Betsey," he said, "what difference does it make how many times you're married? Three? Four? None? Do what you must. Enjoy your life while you have it."

When Betsey says, "Sometimes I think I have Don Juanism, but that's okay with me," she is accepting one of the traditionally "masculine" traits in her personality. In our culture, males are generally assumed to have the right to experience as many women as they wish. This is not only accepted, it is often encouraged and admired. Betsey has co-opted the same rights for herself, regardless of what society—and her one-time therapist—say is good and proper for her as a woman. (Another woman might have acted on the therapist's advice and have been none the happier for it.)

When she approaches a man with the frank statement, "I don't feel like being alone tonight," she runs the risk of rejection. But like so many other sexually aggressive women, her sense of self is so strong that rejection cannot shake it. Instead, she recognizes the possibility that a man's inability to deal with her directness might be his problem.

Betsey's first awareness of her sexual options coincided with her discovering, during her first marriage, that not only did she like sex, she positively thrived on it. It is typical of Betsey that she went out and researched the subject—that she became an amateur sexologist and even studied her own genitals thoroughly. I don't know many women who have done this; it is almost as though a woman's private parts are forbidden even to herself.

Though she wishes it were otherwise, Betsey does not function aggressively in her office. But in view of her determination to go after what she really wants (once she's made the decision that she really does want it), I wouldn't be at all surprised to learn, a few years from now, that she is indeed acting with more force and authority on her job, too.

Lynn

"I can sympathize with how a man feels when a woman turns him down."

Lynn, thirty-two, is about twenty pounds over-weight. She has short-cropped, light brown hair and a voluptuous mouth that is in direct contrast to the serious, no-nonsense expression she normally wears. Lynn is not lacking in humor, as I found out, but she does not view life as an amusement. Rather, it is something to be worked at.

Divorced after five years of marriage, Lynn now lives with a man whom her four-year-old daughter calls "my almost-Daddy."

One day, I was talking numbers of lovers with a friend, who was crowing because he'd just broken the one hundred mark, and I said "Wow, I have a long, long way to go." It's been twenty-some for me, I guess, but I don't chalk up records. That's a male game I won't play. But I'm sexually aggressive, if you call being straightforward and direct aggressive.

If I like a man, I say so. If he doesn't reciprocate—it doesn't have to be *verbal*, but I look for *some* kind of feedback—I don't pursue it. I'm not a masochist. I'm not terribly sensitive, either, but I don't want to be hurt. I can sympathize with how a man feels when a woman turns him down.

Sex was something I saved for my husband during most of my marriage. It lasted five years and it was devastating when we separated. Steve and I lived together before we were married. We seemed to be in tune emotionally, sexually, all ways. But it was all downhill from the minute the ring went on.

The first inkling of trouble came on our wedding night when he said he was too tired. It was something like "Honey, can't we skip it just this once?" I couldn't believe it! I kept insisting that we *had* to, it was our wedding night. I tried to arouse him ... I went down on him. But he simply wasn't having any. I couldn't understand it and I still don't.

How can anyone explain a situation where you have sex twice a day when you're living together, and then once every two weeks after the ceremony? I don't need sex twice a day. I never did. But the extremes to which our relationship went were incredible.

He didn't want to talk about it. Obviously, he had a serious hangup, but he refused to see a therapist.

Now ... since we'd been having perfectly super sex before the wedding, and since *I* hadn't changed, I knew the problem had to be *his*. I'd been in therapy for a while, and, in the fourth year of our marriage, when there was a *six-month* stretch with no sex, my therapist turned to me one day and asked what I was going to do about it. I decided on divorce.

Even with all the divorces today, I was shaken by the split. I did not take it in stride the way some people do—or at least seem to. I felt committed to Steve and I tried everything I knew, from saying, "Let's fuck, I'm horny," to dancing around in bras and bikini pants, to cuddling up next to him while we were listening to music.

Then I tried letting him come to me, but I waited once for three weeks and nothing happened, and I've got stronger needs than that.

But, still ... it was a long time before I went outside the marriage. Instead, I'd use my own hand to relieve the tension.

Eventually, I felt so deprived, so starved for human warmth, that other men began to look appealing. I began to fantasize about men I saw in the street. Even the mailman looked good.

One night, at a party, I met someone who seemed to want to be friendly with both Steve and me, as a couple. He was attractive and I went all out to be charming and funny. I found myself inviting him to dinner.

The three of us became quite close. We had dinner together, went to the movies, we even went sailing one weekend. We were quite the threesome. On the surface, it was all very innocent. But I was getting very hot for this man, Ron. I kept it to myself. At the same time, back in my own bedroom, I was still unsuccessfully trying to arouse Steve.

Then Ron signed a lease on a new apartment and I volunteered to help him move in. It was the first time we'd been alone. It was a hot day and he wore no shirt. After ten minutes of unpacking dishes and hanging up clothes and watching the muscles in his arms and back, I stepped out of my clothes.

He looked at me in ... it was something like shock. "Please don't do this," he said.

My heart was pounding. My underpants had been all sticky—I wanted him so much. I felt like a fool standing nude in front of him while he rejected me, but I managed to ask him whether he was afraid of Steve.

I tried to tell him it'd be okay, but he was still either frightened or not aroused. So I went to him and ground my body into his. I just wouldn't, *couldn't* be refused.

He finally did get an erection and I pulled him down onto the bare floor with me and we screwed among the packing crates. I was so pent up after months of abstinence that after the first orgasm, I asked him to satisfy me three times orally.

It was a totally new way for me to act, and the sex was very, very good. We slept together until after my divorce, which came about a year later. All that time, believe it or not, I was still doing whatever I could to hold the marriage together. I wanted to be a good wife and mother and I reasoned that with outside sex, the marriage could last.

But it didn't; both of us became increasingly angry. We found out we couldn't talk about anything.

The end of the marriage seemed like the end—period—to me. I was shattered. Sex with Ron was one of the things that sustained me. I used it like medicine, to make me feel better.

I knew from my experience with Ron that I could always have men if I wanted them. And I did. I began to take the initiative. Never with husbands of friends, though. I despise messy situations.

I don't care about a man's looks as long as he's not too fat or otherwise repulsive. But I don't want someone who's inhibited in bed. I've had a couple of men past thirty-five who seemed to think the missionary position is the only one there is. There was another man, in his forties, who objected to my language. He said it was unladylike to use words like "fuck" and "cunt." Need I add that he was an unimaginative, uptight lover?

I watch out now for men with hangups. Sometimes I talk about what I want to do in bed *before* we get there. That way everybody knows where everybody stands. Most men are turned on by sex talk. The ones who aren't usually are the uptight ones I don't want, anyway.

Sometimes I love to sit on top and talk and tell him I love feeling his big fat cock inside me, and that it's juicy and delicious. Other times, I prefer to concentrate on the feeling and not say anything at all.

I don't like anal sex. It hurts, so it turns me off. Nothing is fun if it hurts.

Usually, I have one orgasm. I don't come and come and come. I never met a woman who did, but I've read about it.

We have an understanding, my current lover and I, that we will not discuss other sexual experiences if we have them. I told him that even if I ask, not to give in and tell me. This is the only rule we have.

Yes, I'd be terribly jealous if I felt he were emotionally involved with another woman. But, no, I don't mind if he occasionally sleeps with someone else. My feeling is, "God bless you ... have a good time ... give her one for me."

In the beginning, he—his name is Howard—demanded fidelity. Then, one day about six months after he moved in with me, he came in and said, apropos of nothing, "You know, I was married fifteen years. I didn't play around. I missed out on a lot of good sex. I was an idiot. Let's both give ourselves the freedom to move around a little."

I looked him straight in the eye and said, "Good for you, Howard. I'm glad you can finally admit what you want."

The couple next door were swingers—they actually called themselves "swingers"—and one day they invited Howard and me to join them. We discussed it. I didn't like the man. He's your typical male chauvinist pig who acts like he owns his wife. But I was curious. Up till then I'd had only straight one-to-one sex. So we accepted.

I'd never been with a woman, so I started out with the husband. Half-jokingly, I said something like "I'm going to fuck you good ... I'm going to do the job right." He cracked up and said I sounded like dialogue in a bad porno book.

I went down on him anyway, but he made no move toward me. I said, "Hey, you can't leave me hanging ..." His answer was "I'm fussy about whom I eat, lady." I got up and walked out. That was the end of group sex for me.

My childhood? Ordinary. With an ordinary, nice, uptight woman for a mother. She never said it in so many words but she managed to get the message across that "nice" girls submit to their husbands, but they never actually enjoy sex. You can imagine how confused and guilty I felt when I discovered that, even though I wasn't supposed to, I loved sex. That was good for many hours with my shrink.

It's going to be different for my daughter. I want her to be able to take care of herself, enjoy herself in all ways, to make her own decisions and not to feel she's a second-class citizen because she's female.

She already asks about sex, and I answer her simply and honestly, but only what I think a four-year-old can absorb.

She understands that my lover is sort of "like a Daddy," but she doesn't know about the other men because I don't bring them home.

Recently she asked if she could watch us making love. I said it was a private thing, and she'd know what it was like for herself when the time came. But I was happy she asked, because I remember wanting to ask my parents the same thing when I was little, but I never felt free enough to do it.

Some of the things I've said here have been on my mind forever and forever. I've unloaded an awful lot. It's a wonderful feeling to talk about these things and to know I'm not getting a good or a bad check mark because of my behavior.

Lynn lived much of her life as a victim of circumstances. Her uptight mother implied that it was bad to enjoy sex—leaving Lynn with no choice but to feel that she, herself, was bad when she discovered that she did indeed enjoy it.

Lynn was victimized, too, in her relationship with her. I could guess at the underlying causes for his lack of interest in sex after marriage, but the realistic burden it imposed on her was intolerable to the point that—even though she wished to be a good wife and mother—she finally had to seek release elsewhere.

That she emerged as a whole, functioning human being is certainly in part attributable to her years spent in therapy. But sex, too, had something to do with it. As she herself says, "Sex was one of the things that sustained me. I used it like medicine, to make me feel better."

Lynn is probably capable of entering into productive long-lasting relationships, but she is not ready for total commitment and perhaps she never will be. I doubt that she will ever again hand over control of her life into another person's hands.

She has gone past subterfuge. She is honest about her relationship with Howard, the primary man in her life. She acknowledges that she may take other lovers, but that when she does, she will not discuss them with him. She expects the same consideration from Howard. She admits that her lack of jealousy extends only to sexual encounters, not to emotional involvements. And for the time being, that is the extent to which she can handle her new freedoms.

Edith

"The sexual experimenting I should have been doing in my twenties, I'm doing now in my late forties."

Edith, forty-nine, is a big woman, tall, with large breasts and hips. Her reddish hair is a bit too bright to pass for the real thing, but everything else about her is natural, warm, easygoing. She has an exuberant laugh and a positive, straightforward way of expressing herself.

Her parents were wealthy and she went to a series of fashionable schools. She says she married her husband because he, too, was rich. Unfortunately, he was also a schizophrenic and the marriage ended in divorce. When I talked with Edith, she had been divorced for four years and separated for nine. She has three children, twenty-three, twenty and nineteen.

There are two kinds of sexual aggressiveness. There's your pre-intercourse attitude, and then there's the way you behave in bed. I would say that my pre-intercourse attitude is particularly aggressive.

At a bar, I'm sometimes very shy and stiff, sitting off in a corner with my little drink in my hand. Other times I'm quite the show-off. I'm a good dancer and I love to be the center of attention. It depends on my mood and the situation.

I look at a man in exactly the same way a man looks at a woman. I assess him: I like lots of hair, broad shoulders, a kind face. I don't like fat men, and I've never been attracted to anyone much younger than myself. When I see someone who looks appealing and who's the right age, and if he's also got a kind of twinkle, a certain sparkle, then I'll march right over to him and say "What's new?"

The first time I acted aggressively was on vacation in Puerto Rico, not long after my divorce. I was lonely and sexually needy.

I found a very ordinary bar, and I'd sit there every night, listening to music and just looking around. After a week or so, I managed to pick up a couple of lowlife guys and I alternated, one on one night, the other the next.

What amazed me was my ability to do it. Being far from home and in the kind of atmosphere where I'd never meet one of my own kind made it easier. Also, I was in very bad shape then, what with the divorce and all. I needed to be reassured of my desirability as much as I needed the sex itself. I needed a man's body around me and inside of me. I needed to smell masculinity.

I remember staying on my own bar stool and calling two stools away to start the first conversation. I made some flip remark like, "Hey, how can we get to know each other when you're there and I'm here?" He immediately moved over and within a few minutes I had come out with the sexual proposition. I actually propositioned him. I said, "Listen, I haven't had any sex for a long time, and you're physically very attractive to me. What do you say?"

That was man number one. A couple of nights later I met man number two the same way.

There is one danger in this. A very real danger. Men are physically stronger than women. Usually, you can tell the crazies after a few minutes of talk, but not always. You can never discount the possibility of getting mixed up with a really violent, nutsy man. But back then I was so hard up I was willing to take my chances.

I wasn't brought up to be sexually aggressive, certainly not to go to bars and pick up men! I certainly had a lot of old hangups to overcome before that time in Puerto Rico. But if you need it badly enough . . .

Now I can be aggressive anywhere. If I go skiing in Vermont, I'll chat with someone on the tow line. Often the men are alone, but they're not single. Usually the wife doesn't ski or they can't get a babysitter so the wife stays home with the kids and the man comes up alone.

When I meet a man and I like him and I think, "This is it," I'll be the one to make the advances. At a bar, I might start rubbing my hand along the inside of his thigh, make some kind of physical contact.

In bed, I feel free to do whatever I want. I also feel free—politely—to refuse to do anything he asks me to do if I don't want to. Like having anal sex or sucking. Funny. Sometimes I love to suck a big prick and other times I'm turned off. So I don't do it. With my husband, I did whatever *he* wanted. I was the good, submissive wife.

I was a virgin when I married. My husband had slept only with prostitutes. He hadn't had an enduring physical relationship with any women that he cared about. In his family, just as in mine, sex was like disease. Nobody from a nice family has diseases—or sex. That was the prevailing attitude.

My husband couldn't hold an erection. It would take him two seconds to come. I knew during all those years that I was missing out on something but I could never figure out what to do about it. I never had an orgasm until after the divorce.

The life I lead now sure is very different from the life I was brought up to live. I go to the movies by myself if I want to. I don't feel I *must* have a date to go out to dinner at someone's house. But if I do want a man, I'll call one up and invite him along.

I've changed my mind about so many things in the last few years! I have different ideas about what's good and what's bad, what's important and what's not.

I think the women's movement is partly responsible. I'm not active in the movement, but I'm interested. I know what it's all about and mostly I agree.

I think simply getting older has changed me, too. Perhaps I've arrived. At twenty-two, there's a lot you don't know about yourself and the world. At forty-nine, well ... you've been around, you know what it's all about, you learn to accept yourself. At least I have.

Maybe part of the change also has to do with the

circumstances of my life. I've been through so much. I lived with a man who was crazy—literally crazy—who was hospitalized on and off for years, and I was miserable even when he wasn't crazy because there was really nothing between us.

I married him because he was rich. Money was important; it was good back then. Sex was something you didn't talk about; as I said, it was bad, or at least not important. Well, that's all bullshit. My kids are important. My friends are important. Being a good kind human being is important. Fucking is important. Those are my priorities now.

I see my twenty-one-year-old daughter leading a much more independent life than I did. My impulse always was to be independent, but it was so *difficult* back then. Now it's different. Anyway, my daughter has her head together. She knows that sleeping with one man or ten is not the important thing. I encouraged her to sleep with her boyfriend. "Try it," I said. "See if it's any good. Decide your relationship on a lot of things, including sex."

I spend a lot of time with my kids and their friends. I see the books they read. I hear them talk. I find myself picking up some of their language. They're different from the friends I had when I was growing up. The things that are important to them are different. Honesty ... being yourself ... doing something worthwhile ... and, yes, sex.

Some of the freedom of being a young person today has rubbed off on a middle-aged person: me. The sexual experimenting I should have been doing in my twenties, I'm doing now in my late forties.

I don't think my aggressiveness has turned many

men off, but maybe my independent attitude has. I'm aggressive not just in sex, but in my whole life-style. I speak out. I make my presence felt.

I've known a few impotent men, but I really don't believe their impotence had anything to do with my aggressiveness; they would have been impotent with anyone.

One man would get an erection and then lose it. Nothing I did—sucking, stroking, rubbing his penis against my breasts—made any difference. Another man was like my husband; he'd come immediately as soon as he got it in. And then I knew a guy who drank too much. That can be a problem, too. I just run away from all that. Who needs it?

I must say, I used to think it's easier for women. We can fake it if we want to. But once I faked an orgasm and I got caught. The man said, "You're not liquid, you're not wet enough to have an orgasm." I was humiliated. I had to admit the truth and from then on I've seen to it that I do have an orgasm. I'll just ask the man to masturbate me if I don't come during intercourse. I've decided that's okay. Any way you can make it is okay.

Yes, I would like a permanent relationship. I've had a couple that lasted six or eight months and then just gave out. There were never any arguments or big scenes. They just didn't work.

I know two women my age who married much younger men. Maybe that's another new trend, but I could never do it. I would just worry more over each new line and wrinkle on my face. I wouldn't marry a chauvinist, either. But try to find a fifty-year-old male who isn't a chauvinist to some degree.

The pickings are poor and the crop is lean. I'd rather stay home and watch TV than go out simply for the sake of going out. When I need sex, I can get it, but I won't get married simply to have a warm body in bed with me each night. I'd rather go on living this way.

Edith, who went to all the best schools, whose family was not only wealthy, but belonged to the "right" social set, has done a total about-face. In assessing her former values, she flatly and inelegantly proclaims that it was "all bullshit."

Although she says her impulse was always to be independent—"but it was so difficult back then"—she does not dwell on what might have been. Like the true sexually aggressive woman that she is, she focuses on the realities of the here and now: her children, her friends, her need for the physical release of good sex, her desire for a permanent relationship.

Obviously, she's been greatly influenced by her children and their friends, although she does not live vicariously through them. Neither is she intimidated by youth. Certainly she is not one of those rather pathetic women who are entirely caught up in vain, desperate attempts to prolong their own youth. (She would not, for example, enter into a relationship with a much younger man as some of her friends have done.) On the contrary, she seems pleased to have arrived at the age of forty-nine and to be functioning as her own true self at last.

Although it was the trauma of divorce and her need to be reassured of her own desirability that motivated her first aggressive actions in Puerto Rico, the real turning point came when she was accused of faking an orgasm. "I was humiliated," she says. The incident was never repeated and Edith now feels free enough to ask a man to masturbate her to orgasm if she doesn't reach a climax during intercourse.

Like many of the older women, she yearns for a long-term relationship. But she is now a selective, sexually aggressive woman who will not settle for less than she feels she deserves.

Nancy

"I guess you could call me a semi-swinger."

Nancy, thirty-four, is a tall woman with enormous breasts and slim hips and legs. Her hair is dark brown and straight, parted in the middle. She wore no makeup when we met, and her skin showed an occasional blemish. Her voice is deep and her Midwestern background shows in the twang of her speech. Like so many of the other women I talked with, she admitted to being nervous at the beginning of the interview.

Nancy is separated from her accountant husband. She is presently unemployed. She says she plans to look for a job soon.

My father was a fireman. He died fighting a fire and I have the award hanging over my mantel. He was okay. I loved him, but he drank a lot. His big excitement was fighting fires and I'll bet he was glad he died that way . . .

I was brought up strict. Real religious. My mother always told me sex was dirty. She didn't call it sex straight out. She said, "Never let the boys touch you. It's a dirty, filthy thing they want."

She never told me about menstruation. When I

got my first period I didn't know what it was. I thought maybe I'd hurt myself. I was afraid to go to my mother because the blood was coming from down there and she might be angry. I told my girlfriend and she explained what it was all about.

I stayed away from boys until I was eighteen. My first date was with this fellow and I thought I loved him, so I let him go all the way. He got me pregnant and we got married. I never stepped out on him when we were together.

He was strange. A couple years after we got married, he began to like women's underpants. He wore them around the house. Sometimes he would sit and wear them and rub himself until he came. He liked it better than doing it with me. It was creepy to watch him.

I think a sexually aggressive woman is someone who likes doing it, goes after it, and has a lot of orgasms.

I guess you could call me a semi-swinger. I have a steady boyfriend and we swing together. We belong to a swinging club and we meet people through the club, or else our friends bring new people around.

As a member, you tell exactly what you're looking for in sex. You give your age, you describe yourself, what your measurements are, and then they tell you where to write to get in contact with other swingers. They don't give out your phone number unless you tell them it's all right. My phone number is not in the book and I don't give it out much because I've had some crank calls.

I get a lot of requests through the club because of my measurements. Most girls envy me because I have big breasts. I'd rather have a smaller bust, firmer and more evenly proportioned to my body. I'm a 44-DD and blobby. I've done exercises and everything else to get where I want to be, but I can't change my bust size. I've had men who like to put their thingies between my breasts and finish off that way.

Swingers are clean people. We always watch out for VD. A girl can get a heavy discharge, lots of mucus. She's swollen and sometimes there are little bitty yellow pimples, but sometimes you can't see it. I learned recently from a doctor that often women have VD that can't be detected. I'm frankly more concerned now about biswinging than I used to be. A guy would have a discharge and maybe a swelling. I never say, "Okay, boy, lie down. I want to examine you." But I try to get a good look before things go too far.

Jimmy [her boyfriend] and I were with a new couple last night. Somebody said, "Let's quit the chit-chat and get down to the nitty-gritty." We all took off our clothes and sat down on the floor. I took the other fellow and Jimmy took the girl. We had French sex—that's oral sex—and American sex—regular. Then the two fellows got together and I did the girl . . .

With the fellow, I started working down his body with my tongue and when I got to his private area I put it in my mouth. Then we turned around and did 69, with him on the bottom and me on the top. Then we went into intercourse.

With the girl, I started necking with her first . . . rubbing her breasts and then sucking on them. I worked my way down until I got where I wanted to be and then I did her first and we ended in 69.

I like doing it with a girl. It's different. I like men fine, but I don't trust them implicitly. I don't put all my feelings into it because I think they're going to put one over on me. I have more trust in a woman. We can talk better.

A lot of women tell me their problems. I'm a Scorpio, which means I stay calm, and they know they can tell me anything and it won't go any further.

Sometimes they ask me about personal hygiene and sometimes about their problems with their boyfriends. Like if a guy would do something way out ... putting clamps on a girl's breast, or clamps on her private area to spread it wide open ... things like that. Sort of a form of torture. A girl might ask me what to do about it and so forth.

I have one fantasy I haven't done yet. I'd like to get together with about four or five girls and take turns doing each one and then have them all do it to me. Then I'd watch two of the girls together.

I know some girls who say they like to do it with animals. I've only seen it once. It was a girl with a German shepherd and that dog was trained and did it real well. It satisfied her completely and I guess it got satisfied too, the way it appeared. But that's not for me.

I wouldn't like spreading anything on a person, either, or B&D [bondage and discipline]. Some people like to urinate or move their bowels on a person, depending on the situation. B&D is when you're tied up and spanked or hit. You get bitten or hit with a strap. I had an experience where I was with a girl and a fellow who tied me up and I was quite sore afterwards because they got so rough.

Doing it with a girl is as way-out as I go. I used to be afraid to tell people I was bi [bisexual] but things are changing. I see that from reading books and magazines ...

I would never go to a public bar to meet a man, like some women do. I think it's degrading to a woman. If a girl has to go to a bar to pick up a fellow, she's not too much. Also, at a bar, you never know what kind of people you could get mixed up with. Now, with the club, you know the people are going to be the kind you want to be with. You can have a real conversation.

Jimmy and I get together with about twelve other people now. That's our regular group, but we usually don't see them all at the same time. Some are salesmen, some of them are married to people who don't swing, some are couples.

The largest group was ten couples. We sat around and talked. I don't drink but some of the others did. One of the fellows started to get playful and it was time to get undressed. We had a daisy chain. That's where everybody is in a circle ... a fellow and a girl, a fellow and a girl, one after the other. The girl will do the fellow in front of her, and that fellow will do the girl in front of him, and so forth. Everybody moans and groans. That's part of it.

When I'm with my boyfriend alone, I start the sex. I blow in his ear, kiss him, hug him, play with his thingie.

For me, coming is not as strong as a climax. I don't feel it all over my body like a climax. I *come* a lot of times, and the feeling is just down there, but I have a complete climax only once or twice a night. That's the difference. It's the only way I can describe it.

Sure I've noticed a difference in men. Some of them hold back ... you can come three or four times before they do. Some are the opposite. They can't control themselves and they come right away. With a fellow like that, you have to ask him to rub you or use his tongue. Otherwise, you're left with that up-in-the-air feeling.

I can tell a man what to do to make me come. And a woman, too. French sex ... with the tongue ... is what gets me off best.

I was with a fellow who thought the faster he moved his tongue the more satisfied I would be. It's not that way with me and I told him so. He didn't want to listen, but I made him. I told him not all women wanted the same thing. Then he asked me what *I* wanted. I said, "Slow down, take your time, try different things and you'll see for yourself." When he started using his tongue in a slow, soft way, I went off like a cannon.

I used to have guilty feelings about what I do. I was raised to be a different kind of person. But now I don't see what's so wrong with liking sex and swinging if the people you're with want it as much as you do.

In enjoying her special form of aggressiveness, swinging, Nancy has completely renounced her mother's precepts that sex is a dirty, filthy thing. Originally, when she first entered the swinging scene, she says, she experienced feelings of guilt. But the reality of her enjoyment, plus her rationalization that it can't be wrong if the people you're with want it as much as you do, enabled her to overcome those feelings—at least on a conscious level.

Still, I sense a defensiveness in her attitude, which may be due in part to her feelings that I might not approve of her activities. I think it's more likely, though, that Nancy continues to experience conflict at a deeper level. She is, for example, very eager to point out that swingers are "very clean people." And there is a certain self-righteousness in the statement that she would never go to a public bar to meet a man—"If a girl has to go to a bar to pick up a fellow, she's not too much." Nancy's defensiveness may also be due to her untrusting attitude toward men. A woman who is unable to trust any man may be sexually aggressive, but she isn't truly liberated. Certainly, not every man should be put into her "fear" category.

I was intrigued by the fact that though her behavior is freer than that of many of the women I spoke with, her language is quite inhibited. Where other women make casual use of words like "cock," "prick" and "penis," Nancy says "thingie."

Although she does not appear to be totally at ease with the idea of herself as swinger ("I was raised to be a different kind of person") the price she pays for her enjoyment is relatively small in comparison to the pleasure it affords her. And, like the true sexually aggressive woman she is, she does not allow her upbringing or the current mores of the culture to interfere with expressions of her sexuality.

Sharon

"Sex is no problem. Everybody's looking for it. It's there if you know how to get it."

Sharon, forty-seven, has a crop of short, crisp dark curls and brown-black eyes that crinkle at the corners when she smiles, which is often. Of medium height, she has a wiry, athletic-looking body. She speaks rapidly in clear, assertive tones. When she talks, she uses her hands for emphasis, gesturing, stabbing home a particularly important point.

She is head bookkeeper for a large manufacturing firm. Seven years ago, she divorced her husband of twenty years, a man she describes as "worthless, a drinker, an all-around responsibility." Her two children, eighteen and nineteen, support themselves.

I know that a lot of people think of me as an aggressive, dominating person and I have to try real hard not to be too bossy. I like to talk about myself. Monopolize the conversation. But as far as sex goes, I don't usually discuss it.

My upbringing? Well, I had a normal childhood, I guess. Mom brought me up to get married, be a good wife, keep the house clean. All the usual things. Frankly, I loved being a housewife and being with the kids when they were little. I wouldn't have

111

done it any other way. I mean, I was never bitter about staying home like some of the young girls are now.

But I didn't get much sex when I was married. See, my husband, Sam, drank a lot, and he'd come home wanting to screw but usually he couldn't get it up, and then he'd get nasty and blame me. After a few years of that, I'd get up and sleep on the sofa in the living room when he came home drunk.

Honestly, it never occurred to me to cheat on him. It wasn't something I felt I could do. I didn't have the time. I was all wrapped up in the children and I didn't think it would be nice. I mean, the mother of two kids is not supposed to go out and screw around, right? I guess you could say I put sex away in a little dark corner of my mind and closed it off. Oh, I had a few orgasms along the way, but mostly sex—when we had it—was for Sam.

Then came the divorce and after that I went to work. I was busy finding out what the business world was all about. Trying to get ahead. I just knew I could do well, and I did. I started out as a file clerk. Then I took some night courses in bookkeeping. I was a natural. I got promoted fast.

After a while, I felt more relaxed in the office. I began to look around. Up until then I hadn't paid much attention to the people there. I started noticing what went on.

I don't know if it was a typical office scene, or what, but everyone was playing games. The secretaries, the bosses, the salesmen, the mailroom clerks. They were all teasing. Flirting. I didn't know the score then. I thought flirting was all there was to it. I found out different when I got friendly with a couple of the women and they filled me in on who was sleeping with who . . . or is it "whom"?

My mind started to work. There was so much sex in that office you could practically smell it. It was like watching somebody eating cherry pie. All of a sudden I got hungry. I wanted some for myself. But I didn't know how to get it. And anyway, when it came right down to it, most of the men in the office were younger. I've never been interested in younger men. That's not my style.

I decided I'd have to find a man, but I was not going to go after any of those young guys.

One day I was going through the newspaper and I saw an ad for a singles club. I just picked myself up and went. It was a madhouse. Loud music, people dancing, talking. But everyone was young. I felt uncomfortable. I sat there anyway, had a drink, started talking to the bartender. He leaned over and said, "Hey, you know, you're in the wrong place. Try club XXX. They're more your style."

I'll always remember that guy, because if he hadn't told me about the other place, I would have felt so let down, I'd have gone home and stayed there.

The next weekend I tried the new place. It was a madhouse, too, but the music was different and the people looked like my kind of people—my age, everybody neat, no dungarees, no longhairs.

There were a lot more women there than men. I had expected that, but these women looked like such losers. That bothered me. I thought to myself, "They're hard up. That's what it means when you come to a place like this. You're hard up. It's degrading. It's not for you, Sharon. Go on home and be lonely."

But you see, I'm stubborn, and I didn't go home. Instead, I made a little promise to myself: stay here tonight, and if nothing happens, never come back. So I sat down at the bar and put on my best smile.

I heard the bartender say to one of the women, "Not getting any meat tonight?" I couldn't believe it. And he was right, the place was a meat store. People sitting around being looked over like pork chops on a tray. Only nobody was selling. They were giving themselves away.

I sat there for a long time and nothing happened. The next night, I broke my promise and went back. Within half an hour, I met a man. He was sitting across the bar. I liked his looks, so I went over to him and said, "Aren't you a friend of ... ?" The oldest line in the book, but it still works. We started talking and I asked him back to my place for a drink.

That was it. We went together for a year. We did everything together. We had sex in every way, shape and form. We'd screw for hours at a time. He'd do what he wanted and I'd go along with it. Then I'd do what I wanted and he'd go along.

I learned a lot with Hal and that came as kind of a surprise. Sex with my husband was not the greatest but I thought I'd done everything I was capable of doing. Not so.

I was an uptight wife. I had never, never touched my husband's cock. But with Hal, I could do anything. I could stroke and suck and lick his cock and rub it over my eyes—anything.

I felt good with him. I began to feel like my real self. It was like down underneath the Sharon that was a divorced wife, a mother, and a bookkeeper, there was another Sharon who could enjoy herself.

The reason I broke up with Hal? This is going to sound funny, but he wanted me to marry him. He insisted on it. This big, lovable, sexy guy, he was a religious man and he wanted to make an honest woman of me. Except for the thing with me, he lived a very straight life.

I couldn't marry him. I was married for twenty years, and I've had it with pleasing a man and always being told what to do. I want to run my own life.

In the last couple of years, I've dumped three men. Nice men. Like Hal. But the wrong kind for me.

The wrong kind is someone who wants to dominate and thinks being a man gives him the right to tell me what to do. Maybe another kind of man—somebody who'd leave me alone and I'd leave him alone but we'd still be together and love each other—maybe I could marry that kind of man.

After I broke up with Hal, it was ... well, I'd gone from mucho sex to nothing, and I was climbing the walls. I tried masturbating, rolling my finger around, touching myself. I'd never done *that* before. It's nice. I like it, but it's not as good as a man. I need a warm body.

So I keep going back to the singles place, even though I hate it.

Whenever I see someone who looks like a possibility—presentable, decent clothes, a nice smile—I go into my routine. My "rain dance." I'll walk over and start talking. Nothing brilliant—you don't have to be smart or funny—just, "Hi, how are you? What's your name?" I move in close. Laugh. Pay attention to what he's saying. Maybe slide my hand over his, lean against him, whisper something in his ear.

There's no special person in my life right now. Oh, I go out a lot to the bars and clubs. Sex is no problem. Everybody's looking for it, so it's there if you know how to get it. I sleep with this one and that one. It's fun.

But I'd like something special. Not marriage, understand? Not that. I don't want to give up what I've got now ... the freedom. I don't want to share my life. But a special person, you know ... someone I can feel close to.

My talk with Sharon ended on this rather poignant note—a note that was struck time and again during the interviews, especially the ones with the older women.

Many of these women are particularly wary of commitment. They see marriage, and, by extension, even any close semi-permanent relationship, as they were brought up to see it: two people turned in on one another, bound together in mind and body, dependent on each other for all their pleasure. No one was talking of open marriage or alternative lifestyles when they were growing up. So, for them, marriage (or marriage as they've known it) is a step in the wrong direction, a regression to a former, dependent state, a threat to their new freedom.

Sharon and others like her value freedom. But there is also a longing for closeness and companionship. The two are not necessarily mutually exclusive, but it is never easy to strike a balance.

Commitment to another human being does limit the number of ways one can assert one's self. And yet to live without it is to be cut off from some of life's greatest joys. I suppose the most important thing is to avoid getting locked in so growth is impossible—and to remember that inevitably there will be times in any life when closeness takes precedence over freedom and other times when freedom will have priority.

Sharon's life alone began when she divorced an irresponsible husband. At this point she either had to make it on her own or go under. Not only did she make it—both on the job and with men as well—she's been reasonably successful, although she is still dependent on singles clubs that she dislikes.

There seems to be a certain correlation between success at sex and work. Not every successful careerist is also a sexually aggressive woman. But the person who, like Sharon, sets out to brave the business world for the first time at the age of forty will probably bring the same kind of courage to a singles bar.

Sharon, like many women alone, didn't begin to discover the joys of sex until she was into her forties. It's interesting, I think, to consider that in 1900 the average woman's life expectancy was somewhere around forty-seven years, while now a woman can be sexually and emotionally reborn at that age.

Marilyn

**"Some men are good lovers . . .
others have no feeling for it.
There's just as much incompetence in sex as in anything else."**

*Marilyn, thirty-five, is a beautiful woman, perhaps
the most beautiful of all the women I met while in-
terviewing for this book. She is tall and slender and
carries herself like a model, with great assurance.
Her hair is a deep honey blonde, parted on the side
and clipped with a simple tortoise-shell barrette. She
speaks softly and calmly, hesitating from time to
time to find just the right word to express a thought.*

*She was married for ten years and has been di-
vorced for five. She lives alone now, in a small apartment that is sparsely furnished but elegant in its
bareness. She works in real estate, selling and manag-
ing properties.*

I remember my childhood as peaceful and quiet.
My parents got along well and they were not at all
strict with me. If anything, I had too little direction.
I did all the things a middle-class WASP child
growing up in the Midwest might be expected to do.
I was taken to Sunday school, but even as a little
girl I knew we just went because it was the "right"
thing to do.

I have an image of men sleeping with whomever

they wish, whenever they wish and I've been trying to operate this way for quite a while myself. Ever since I left my husband. I suppose that makes me sexually aggressive, although I've never used that phrase.

I would say I've slept with ... oh, maybe thirty men. I haven't counted up, but it's many more than five and certainly less than a hundred. I've slept with single men, men who were living with women and a few married men. No, I don't feel guilty about sleeping with a married man. I can't say why, exactly. I just don't.

How do I decide whether or not to sleep with someone? It has to do with physical attraction, although I have no particular type. I don't usually like a man who is very much bigger ... or younger ... or older than I am. Mainly, I'm attracted to men who have a lively interest in sex. Men who *like* women and respond to me as a grown-up, experienced woman, not a girl. I'm not attracted to studs—to overdressed, overbearing glamour boys who fuck up a storm but who are really lousy lovers because they aren't responding to the woman so much as they are to their own bodies.

Sex was part of the reason my marriage went bad. I had orgasms most of the time and by having them I learned that orgasms aren't everything. With Lou [her husband] I suffered from emotional deprivation. I remember crying and not getting any sympathy, baring my soul to him and suddenly realizing that he wasn't listening. He didn't know what I was saying, and he didn't give a damn.

Lou was very successful. He traveled a great deal.

The night I left him, he'd been away for seven weeks. He came home in the afternoon and I left that evening. I was faithful to him even though I had hundreds of perfect opportunities to "cheat" (isn't that a dreadful word?). I didn't take lovers because, if I had, I wouldn't have been able to maintain my own perfect-wife image: beautiful, intelligent, a good hostess, and *faithful*.

I've gone through some definite stages since my marriage broke up. First there was pulling the pieces back together again. Then came realizing who I am and what I really want. The night I decided to leave Lou ... well, what happened is indicative of what was wrong.

But first I want to tell you about something that happened a week before I left. I was listening to the radio—a talk show about encounter groups. Listeners were invited to a session planned for the following weekend at a beach resort not far from the city.

I had never, ever thought about getting involved in an enounter thing, but it sounded interesting and I was lonely and liked the idea of a weekend at the beach, so I signed up.

Although I didn't actually participate by sharing my feelings, I watched everything that happened that weekend. I was moved by the honesty of it all, the way the people opened up to one another. It was beautiful to see how supportive and loving they became. Something in me was deeply touched. At the end of the weekend, the director and I walked along the beach together, and out of nowhere I began to cry—as hard as I can ever remember crying.

It was the first time in my life I wanted to be

dead. I had a vision of the beach empty, deserted. Desolate. Everything bare and dead. I finally came out of it and I said to the director—who had been holding me and stroking my hair all that time—"It's a lie, a lie. I don't want this life. I don't want to be married to him."

That was a turning point. A week later Lou came home. I told him I was unhappy and wanted things to be different. His response was to lead me into the bedroom. I didn't want sex then, but, as usual with Lou, I went along with it. Afterwards, he said, "Whew, I really needed to get my rocks off."

That was it. A steel door clanged shut between us. He didn't care how I felt. He just wanted to get his damn rocks off. I threw some things in an overnight bag, called a friend to say I was coming for the night, and left. I never slept with my husband again.

It took me a year to be able to admit that my marriage had failed and even longer to realize it wasn't my fault. I'd been accustomed to thinking the woman was always to blame when a marriage broke up, that if the wife had been less demanding or more understanding or *something*, things could have been worked out. Now I think a broken marriage means that somebody's moved on.

That's what I did. I see my life as having had a break and then continuing. I was one kind of person until I was eighteen, another kind during my marriage, and I'm a totally different person now.

After the divorce, my first important relationship was with a bisexual man. His thing was sex, like someone else's thing might be wine or sports cars. He writes about it, thinks about it, talks about it and lives it. I learned a lot from him, not just about sex—though that was certainly the basis for our being to-gether—but about people, life, myself, too. I never thought we'd stay together longer than a couple of years, but while it lasted it was very good. I date my aggressiveness from that time.

It was wild. We traveled to California and Mexico with a group—two other men and another woman. Everybody slept with everybody else, singly and in every possible combination.

I was less aggressive with two men than with one. But I'd usually arrange the fucking position. I might suck one man and have the other suck me.

With a woman I'm aggressive, but I'm not com-pletely at ease. I've never had oral sex with a woman but I've brought them to climax by masturbation, and I've been masturbated but not to climax.

When I'm with a woman and a man and the man and I are fucking, I try to maintain some contact with the woman, hold her hand or caress her breast—a kind of I'm-not-forgetting-you thing.

Since those crazy days, I'm sexually more de-manding and less accepting. I don't even pretend that I've enjoyed sex if I haven't—something I used to do with Lou. If the sex is bad and the man is someone I'm not especially interested in, I won't sleep with him again. If I do like the man, I show him how to make me come.

I grew up thinking that all men just somehow "know" how to make love and that if I didn't come there was something wrong with me. Now I know better. Some men are good lovers, skillful and also very giving in an emotional sense—like my bisexual friend—and others have no feeling for it. There's just as much incompetence in sex as in anything else. And, God knows, there's a lot of incompetence around.

I said before that I'm more demanding now and more critical. But I hope I've never been cruel or unkind. I try not to be. One man, someone I've known for a while and am very fond of, had trouble getting an erection the first time we slept together. He's very slender, not physically strong, and his penis is very small. I was so *unworried*, so relaxed and casual about it, that within an hour he was very hard and the sex was good. I know I'm attractive and my confidence seemed to help.

I don't live with anyone now, but when and if I decide to, I'd want the man to share the housework. And I mean *half* of it, not just a part of it as a "favor" to me. I'm interested in a man as a sex partner and as a person who is together and mature. Not a little boy who can't take responsibility for his clothes and food and cleaning up after himself. I earn my own money, so I don't expect a man to take care of me, either. My ideal is total sharing.

Once, after my bisexual friend and I broke up, I had a part in a pornographic movie. It was not pleasant. There was a great deal of pressure on everyone to perform. Especially the men. You have to have "come shots"—that's what they call the scenes where the man ejaculates. It wasn't fun. There was no tenderness.

Thirty men after my marriage, I want one good relationship. I've come full circle, but now I know myself and what I want.

Marilyn grew up with a veritable catalog of cultural misconceptions. Experience, along with a rapidly-emerging sense of self, has helped her to be free of many of them.

At one time she felt (as do many women) that the wife is to blame when a marriage fails—that things can almost always be worked out if the woman is less demanding, or more understanding, or something. Now, because of her own situation, she sees divorce as an indication that somebody's moved on.

She has also assumed (again, like many women) that men just somehow "know" how to make love; that if she didn't achieve orgasm, it was her fault. Now, after sex with many, many men, she says, "There's just as much incompetence in sex as in anything else," and she refuses to sleep twice with any man who proves an insensitive, incompetent lover.

But though Marilyn is selective, she is also sensitive to the needs of others. (Sensitivity is traditionally a feminine quality, but I see it as one of the better human qualities—one that does not necessarily interfere with or cancel out an individual's aggressiveness.) When Marilyn slept with an old friend and found him impotent, she was kind, patient, and confident of her own sexuality. The man relaxed enough to achieve erection, and she reports that the sex was very good.

Marilyn is objective about herself. She views her life as a series of stages: a peaceful, quiet childhood; a marriage during which she felt compelled to maintain a perfect-wife image; a period of questioning followed by a painful divorce; a time of experimentation and getting to know her true self;

and now, the search for one good relationship. Implied throughout Marilyn's story is an awareness and acceptance of change within herself. Such women never grow old. They grow.

Joan

"Sex is nature's tranquilizer."

Joan, thirty-two, bounced into my office looking like the star player on a girls' school hockey team. Her face is round, her eyes very blue and frank, her skin fresh and healthy-looking. She has a plump body and when I met her the lower half was tightly encased in jeans, while the upper was snugged into a t-shirt at least two sizes too small. She speaks quickly in a high, lilting voice and she almost always smiles.

Brought up in a solidly middle-class Midwestern family, Joan married young, was divorced at thirty and now teaches English in a junior high school.

Hi. I was really looking forward to this. Where shall I begin? [I told her she could start wherever she wanted, and she launched into the following monologue.]

Well, I *love* sex. I think sex is nature's tranquilizer. It makes me feel good. I need it for release. I like to get laid now and worry about problems later. I work hard, because my ex gives me nothing for support. But that's okay. I can manage.

Listen, women have to do their thing. I was talking to a friend who's still in graduate school. She says she's too busy to look for a man. I told her, "Forget about a relationship until you get your degree ... just go out and get laid the way I do." She screamed at me, "Joan, I could *never* do that."

Well, I couldn't convince her and that's okay, too. Like they say, different strokes for different folks.

I'm a feminist and what that really means is that I'm for women. I respect them and I respect myself. I'll never be a shitworker for a man, sexually or any other way.

The attitude I've seen in women, and in myself in the past, is that we'd better not approach the men because they might not like it. I wonder if they ever think *we* might not like being approached. Probably not. They just assume we do. I think we're also afraid they might not want us the way we really are. I've got broad hips, occasionally there's a pimple on my ass. I'd get uptight about me. I'd want to be the way I thought they wanted me to be. Well, fuck that. I'm me.

I've always come on strong. That's the truth about me. People always thought of me as aggressive. For a long time it didn't bother me at all.

That was my tomboy stage. When I got into later adolesence, I had the feeling my social life wasn't quite what I wanted it to be. I never let on about this. I always made sure my façade was firm and tight.

I started fucking at fifteen with a boy I met at school. He was a kid and probably nervous about getting laid. A premature ejaculator, but I didn't even know what to call it then. The sex was lousy but I pretended it was great. I didn't want to hurt his feelings and anyway I had what every girl in school wanted: a boyfriend, a lover.

By the time I went off to college I was fucking regularly and having orgasms all over the place. I met my husband my first week on campus. He was sitting in the snack bar. I noticed him because he's tall and thin and I've always liked tall, thin men. I wonder . . . is that because I'm short and fat?

I went back the next day and he was there again. I walked up and said, "Hi, I saw you here yesterday. Do you come here often?" We talked—or rather, I talked. He—his name is Jerry—didn't say much. I suggested that we go for a walk. It was cold and my teeth were chattering, so he offered me his jacket and a ride back to my dorm. As I was getting out of the car, I let my hand rest on his knee for just a second or two and said, "Do you feel like a movie tonight?"

He did and we went. Afterwards, as we sat in the car in front of my dorm, I cuddled up next to him. He sat stiff, like a stone. I had a flash of insight: it wasn't that he wasn't interested; he was *scared*. I thought to myself, "My God, I've got a virgin." I found out later that I was right.

I moved very close and kissed him. He didn't know what to do with his mouth; his lips were tight and pursed together in a prissy way.

But I liked him and thought it might be fun to initiate him—woman-of-the-world that I was, what with all my previous experience. So I asked him out on another date. He didn't know it, of course, but he was going to get fucked the next time.

After that next date, I maneuvered him back to his apartment. We sat down on the sofa and I began to climb all over him in a playful way. I put my arms around his neck and pressed my nose against his, making sure that my breasts grazed his chest. I can be very cute when I want to be and he couldn't *not* put his arms around me when I was being so snuggly. Pretty soon he was breathing hard and there was a nice point in his pants.

We necked for a little bit and I undressed myself, finally, since he didn't make any motions in that direction. I lay down on the sofa and pulled his head down to my breasts. I took his hand and pressed it to my cunt and soon the inevitable happened.

But I didn't have an orgasm and I was wild to have one, so I showed him how to masturbate me.

He got to be a pretty good lover and we kept screwing during the three years we went together before our marriage. We were married five years and the sex was always at least okay and sometimes sensational.

During the time we were together, when I wanted sex I'd just go over to him, put my hand on his penis and hold on, or unzip him and wait until it got hard. I usually wanted it more than he did.

Jerry was very well aware that I am ... ahem ... highly sexed, and his favorite strategy when he was angry, was to refuse to fuck. When he started with this little trick, the marriage began to fall apart.

Now I live with a forty-year-old man. We have a

completely sensual thing going. I've found my mate. I love everything about him, his odors, even his farts.

Joe was the victim of what he calls an "uptight marriage to an uptight wife." He thinks I'm great because uptightness was never one of my problems. He likes it when I'm aggressive and he says it turns him on when I take over and direct our lovemaking.

I can't imagine not telling a man exactly how to please me. If he's eating me, I'll say more pressure, less pressure, up here, down there. I tell him if I want his tongue in my cunt, on the tip of my clit, or even in my anus. I don't usually use such a clinical word. Asshole is more like it.

But, sure, he does the same with me. I expect him to.

You probably think from what I've said so far that I want to be on top all the time. Okay, yes, sometimes it's an ego trip. I feel like *I'm* doing it to *him* because I can control the rhythm. When I'm on top he can put his finger on my clit and that's a mind-blower.

I like it from the rear, too, but it doesn't work very well unless he has a really stiff hard-on.

But I'm not always the dominant one. We both like to try new things and he can be very inventive. We talk about our sexual fantasies sometimes, and this can be a big turn-on. It also makes us feel closer.

One of his fantasies is that I'm sitting in my classroom, and he comes in when I'm in the middle of a lesson and masturbates me in front of everyone.

Then he pushes the chair out of the way, and fucks me from behind.

My fantasy is that I'm twenty pounds thinner and walking in the park in a long chiffon gown. I see him, I pull up my skirt and show him my cunt and then we hit the grass.

When Joe is tired and I'm really horny, I masturbate. It doesn't happen often, but it happens.

I'm totally involved with him. He's a computer expert and I'm interested in his work. He knows how much I love teaching and he encourages me to go back to school for my Master's. I like his friends and we share a few interests, though we're not Siamese twins by any means. We respect our differences. We respect each other.

Doing it with a woman intrigues me, too. I'm curious about how I'd react. It's something I want, but I'm not quite sure how to arrange it. I think it would be easiest in a group situation and Joe and I both are sending out feelers . . .

I'm puzzled. I think of my mother and father living the good life out in the Midwest, with their nice house and polished silver candlesticks—God forbid they should get tarnished—and their simonized Cadillac, and they have what everyone is supposed to want when they get to be in their fifties. And yet they seem so—how can I say it—they seem half-dead. Do they care about each other? I don't know but I bet they haven't screwed in years—at least not each other. Mother's two favorite things are housekeeping and playing tennis, and Dad . . . he probably gets a few bangs on business trips, but is that any kind of a life? It won't happen to me.

I earn my own living and that gives me certain rights. I like that. I'm comfortable not being married; teaching; loving music and nineteenth-century poetry; having good sex. And Joe's happy, too. What else is there?

Joan is, in my opinion, the ultimate sexually aggressive woman. She positively vibrates with energy, enthusiasm, honesty and, yes, sex.

She revels in being herself. She rejects male-defined standards of beauty. "I'm me," she says. I am woman, I am sexual, but I am also me. I conform to my own criteria.

Joan does not imitate men. But her behavior seems manlike because we've come to think of independent, strong, assertive people with positive self-images as being masculine.

"Sex is nature's tranquilizer," she says. "I like to get laid now and worry about problems later." Most people, if they were asked whether the statement was made by a male or female, would guess male. It represents a pragmatic approach to sex that is, again, manlike.

Women are supposed to desire sex most when the relationship is romantic, tender. Joan is less sensitive to the emotional climate; she wants it when she wants it. (Conversely, when Jerry refused her sex because he was angry, he was acting the petulant-woman's role—the wife who turns away from her husband after a spat.)

With characteristic bluntness, Joan says she will not be a shitworker for a man. And she isn't. Her very warm and satisfying relationship with Joe

should offer encouragement to any woman who be-
lieves in the possibility that two human beings can
exist in love and mutual respect with neither doing
the shitwork of the other.

Chapter 4

THE YOUNG SINGLES

Perhaps I imagine it, but it seems to me that fewer and fewer of the songs young people listen to now contain lyrics such as "You belong to me forever," "If you leave me, I'll die," "Now that you're mine I'll never let you go" and the like—the kind of lyrics I grew up with and that always brings to mind images of chains and fetters, being bound hand and foot to some other person through all eternity, like it or not. They were about love, but that love had a desperate, frightened, possessive quality.

The new songs are less romantic, more sexually explicit, and while love is still what most of them are all about, it is a freer, more easygoing emotion that comes across.

I can't help feeling the change is indicative of a change of attitude among the young. In any case, the young, single, sexually aggressive women I spoke with are anything but desperate and possessive about their own love/sex lives. Instead, they conduct their erotic affairs surely, unselfconsciously, and with a spirit of gay adventure.

It is *almost* assumed now that young women in their teens and twenties will have had one or more sexual experiences before marriage (if they do indeed decide to marry). And while these "nice" girls are dabbling in occasional good-old-fashioned heterosexual sex, the sexually aggressive have become true connoisseurs—sampling, comparing, and enlarging their repertoire of sexual behavior in much the same way as a gourmet cook experiments with new ways to prepare fine food.

These young women are critical observers of male bodies and express their preferences in no uncertain terms. Just as some men say they like big breasts with the nipples placed just so, these young women often indicate an equally specific admiration for, say, a tight, small ass, a long penis, etc. Some talk about sure-fire techniques for picking up likely-looking strangers in bars, or on the street. Many engage in sex with a series of partners and are adept at discarding the ones who do not live up to their own high standards of performance. A few are experimenting with group sex, communal living, and bisexuality.

As for this last, I was quite frankly surprised by the number of young women who slept with other women. At first, I thought the sample of my interviewees might be unrepresentative, but as I continued to investigate, also checking current scientific literature, I realized that this style is simply one more manifestation of the adventurous, anything-goes-as-long-as-it-feels-good attitude of the young sexually aggressive woman.

When I discussed female homosexuality with a male psychiatrist (over forty-five) he immediately launched into a discussion of lesbianism and told me that in his opinion, such behavior must be labelled "sick." I tend to be more in agreement with Dr. Lonny Myers, who says, "If not for social brainwashing and cultural taboos, people could relate sexually to people of both sexes." It seems to me that bisexuality is one of the natural consequences of the blurring of society's hitherto rigid sex-role stereotyping. Now there is a slow but steady drift toward androgyny.

The word "androgyny" (from the Greek *andros*—male—and *gyne*—female) suggests the blending of male and female. Many pop idols of the young have an androgynous appeal. Mick Jagger, a sex symbol for *both* sexes, comes immediately to mind. So does the late Janis Joplin (who, not-so-incidentally, is supposed to have been bisexual). The gentle, sensitive male, the strong, assertive female—whatever their sexual predilections—are androgynous; each is imbued with qualities traditionally associated with the opposite sex.

In any event, polarization of the sexes along rigidly defined lines—i.e., passive woman, aggressive man—seems to have resulted in as much grief and discomfort as it has brought pleasure for both females and males. These young sexually aggressive women, in perceiving both men *and* women as sexually appealing *people*, are gaining a new perception of themselves. They may well effect a redefinition of the traditional male—female relationship.

And the traditional female—female relationship may also undergo some changes. Many young women are experiencing more positive feelings about themselves *as* women—an attitude roughly akin to the "black is beautiful" feeling that was actively fostered in the black community not so long ago. In previous eras, many women regarded other members of their sex mainly as competitors—at least until they were safetly married. In a totally male-dominated culture such women often betrayed each other in order to enhance their own chances for a secure niche (marriage) in society. But independent women who can support themselves financially, emotionally, and sexually, and who do not feel that catching a man—any man—is the ultimate goal, can afford to view one another with respect, admiration, and sometimes love. In any case, I have the feeling that woman's hostility toward woman will continue to diminish as more and more females grow into healthy, self-sustaining personhood.

With the exception of Cathy, who appears to be in real trouble, I would not care to predict whether some of the "far out" behavior exhibited by the young singles will end in self-destruction. I do know that in the process of liberating themselves, they are also freeing their men from the heavy burden of traditional *maleness*. The end result *could* be a happy and much longed-for detente between the sexes.

Robin

"I love a long, sensual scene . . . stroking, playing, kissing, listening to music. . . . It could go on for hours."

Robin, twenty-five, is a fragile-looking blue-eyed blonde—the type that was once invariably compared to a Dresden doll. But her style is strictly contemporary. Slender, with a flat, long-legged boyish figure, her eyebrows are tweezed to mere hairline dimensions, her mouth is colored a ripe cherry red, her clothes are the ultimate in funky-chic. Robin works as an airlines reservation agent, lives with two cats in a studio apartment from which furniture—except for a bed—is strangely absent.

She sits quietly in her chair, speaking softly but with determination and with no hint of nervousness in her manner.

I have three crazy brothers, two neurotic sisters, a father with ulcers, a mother who spent the best years of her life doing six loads of wash a day. And now that she doesn't need to anymore she drinks to pass the time. That's my nice middle-class American family.

For a long time I didn't get along with my folks. They lived such a . . . such a *small* life. It was all work, work, work, and God help them if they should ever once enjoy themselves. My mother got the worst of it. She slaved and catered to my father. She still practically bows down when he gets up in the morning.

You'd think she'd want something different—better—for me. But no. She asks, "When are you going to settle down, Robin? When are you going to have a family?" As though there's no other way.

I don't think she really expects an answer anymore. I've been on my own for such a long time now, I think she feels lucky that I'm not strung out on drugs.

I fly out to visit them once a year, at Christmas. But I'm always glad to get back to my own place again. I have a nice life. Good friends. I can travel around a lot because of my job. I meet plenty of men.

My mother would have a heart attack if she knew, but I've been having sex since I was fifteen. The first time was with a kid from school. He put it in and he came. I remember thinking, "Is *this* what it's all about?" It took a couple of years before I had an orgasm, and I couldn't even honestly say I enjoyed sex until, oh ... maybe two years ago. I started to enjoy it at about the same time I became what you call "aggressive."

Now, when I want a man and there's no one special in my life, I go to a bar. I never go alone, ever. I'd feel naked. I go with a girlfriend.

We sit, we have a drink, we look over the scene. We look at guys ... their bodies. I'm really into that now.

I look for men with small, tight asses who are thin

. . . who look *almost* gay, but aren't. I like blond hair, blue eyes, a heavy, strong chin. Occasionally I wind up with a husky, dark, outdoor type. I'm not *that* finicky.

When I spot somebody interesting, I give a quick look to see if he's alone. If he is, I get up and walk over and say, "Hi, how are you?" At the same time, I smile, a mischievous look that means, "*You* know what I want, but let's not be *too* obvious about it."

Then we start talking. If he seems okay—not a moron, not a weirdo—I invite him back to the table where my girlfriend and I are sitting. We talk some more and if for any reason I decide I don't like his style, or his conversation, I signal to my friend and we make up an excuse and leave. Otherwise, I'll invite the guy back to my apartment.

I *always* go to my place. I feel more in control there. I know where everything is, what records I want to play, what we can eat later.

Usually, we sit on the floor and drink wine. There's a natural flow from talk to sex. Often, I'm the one to make the first move. I'll take his hand and put it on my breast. Or I'll lick my finger and rub it on his lower lip. At some point, I stand up and take off my clothes. I don't like to have a guy undress me. It's psychologically bad—"Me Tarzan, you Jane." I lose by it.

One man I know describes his sex as getting a hard-on, putting it in, and getting it over with. I do not sleep with him. I love a long, sensual scene . . . stroking, playing, kissing, listening to music, smoking a joint, eating, more stroking and kissing. It could go on for hours. The atmosphere is *it* for me. It's definitely not just the sex.

I'm in a mood to experiment now. I'm discovering more about myself through sex. I keep seeing myself change. The more I experience, the more aware I become of what it is to be aggressive or passive, in and out of bed. The final results aren't in yet [she laughs] but so far, aggressive is better.

Last winter I met a guy skiing. We talked. I invited him to my room at the lodge. I immediately got on top. I did all the moving and he lay there, very passive. It was a change ... not just physically, but emotionally.

Aggressive doesn't mean using force. It means having some control. There's a difference. I might want a man to suck me. But I wouldn't want him to if *he* didn't want to. And I wouldn't "make" him. How could I?

Sex shouldn't be a war of wills, but sometimes it is. Once, a guy wanted me to suck him to orgasm and then swallow it. I didn't want to. I said, "I'm not up for that now." He put his hand on the back of my neck and forced my head down. I just bounced my head back up and said, "I'll tell *you* when I want to do that."

That was about as rough and nasty as anyone ever got with me. I'm aware that a woman takes a chance when she invites a strange man to her house. Men are stronger. That's a fact. But I'm very psychic with a guy. I've always felt I could control a situation with my head. Once I touch him all over, I get the feeling that I know him very well.

There's one kind of guy I don't like to sleep with—

the all-American businessman. Most of the men I see are artists or creative types or students. They understand me and they like it when I take over.

But the uptight businessman ... one got up and left. Another one—get this—he expected me to cook dinner for him! And he couldn't get it up. I think he was worried about the size of his penis. It was small. But everybody knows that size is not where it's at.

Bodies are important. Smooth, healthy bodies. Okay, if the guy seems to need some assurance about his penis, I'll tell him it's lovely, or the shape is good, or it's a nice color.

Here's something interesting. A lot of the guys I meet have been reading sex books. You can tell because they're hung up on technique, and position. They're afraid you'll think they're incompetent if they do things the easy way. They want to keep changing position ... put your left elbow here and your ass over there ... that kind of thing. I don't like what's not natural and not comfortable. With a guy like this, I say, "Take it easy, let's just do whatever feels nice."

Feeling nice ... that's what it's all about.

I sometimes feel very good with a woman, too. I didn't tell you I'm bisexual, did I?

Often, I'm the leader with a woman. At other times, not. Either way, it's a whole different feeling. After the first time with a woman, I knew in a fantastic new way what it is to have a female body ... two beautiful breasts ... a wet vagina ... all the corners of feelings at the edges of the vagina. Sex with a woman made me think more about femaleness. It made me feel better about being a woman.

I don't see men and women at the same time. I move from one to another and I've had long-term relationships with both but I prefer men—the hardness of them. Going both ways has shown me that.

Once, for about a month, I spent time with a married couple. We all made love together. It was lovely ... a lot of hugging and kissing and licking all around. I liked them both and I would still be with them, except the husband got jealous and broke it up. He decided his wife and I were getting too close; he felt left out. In that situation, I did prefer the woman, but in general, the more experiences I have, the more I know I'm basically heterosexual.

I don't want a life like my parents'. I'll never get married. I think marriage is a ridiculous thing these days. I just see no need for people to go into a "till the day you die" arrangement that leaves no room to move around. Maybe group marriages would be better. Or maybe agreements—contracts—that last for a year and can be renewed if both parties want to.

As for children, there are about a hundred reasons why I don't want them—not now, anyway. The first is that I don't want to get married.

Robin, like so many other young singles, is determined not to live the kind of life her mother had—a "small" life, as Robin describes it, of catering and slaving to a man. So she vows that she, herself, will never get married.

She is especially concerned now with experimenting, growing, changing. ("The more I experience, the more aware I become of what it is to be ag-

gressive or passive, in and out of bed.") Her bisex- uality is in part a result of her desire to know herself better. ("Sex with a woman made me think more about femaleness . . .")

I think Robin will continue to grow and change and—although her sense of self is too strong ever to allow her to fall back into the role of passive, done- to woman—she may in time modify her attitudes about many things. Possibly even including mar- riage.

Ruth

"At the moment, I have two relationships: Valerie for female sex and Bob for male sex."

Ruth, twenty-two, a senior at a large university, looks like the "Daddy's little girl" of another generation. Her hair is red and curly; her white complexion is exquisite and set off by sky-blue eyes and delicately pink cheeks. She has a small, curvy body, and, she told me, she deliberately chooses clothes that show it off.

She talks quickly; one is tempted to say she chatters. She gives the impression of always being in a hurry, even when she's sitting still in a chair. At the same time, she was perfectly at ease during the interview; there wasn't the least touch of self-consciousness about her.

My first sex was here at school, in my freshman year. So you might call me a late bloomer. Most of my friends in high school were doing it at fifteen or sixteen. The joke was, if you were over sixteen you were over the hill. But I wasn't ready at fifteen, and I knew it.

Anyway, I was eighteen, and he was my chemistry professor. A brilliant man, really, but sexually a baby. He would start out by putting his penis in my

148

mouth. Then he would take it out, put it in my vagina, have his orgasm, and go home to his wife.

I've always masturbated, so I knew about orgasms, and I thought I ought to be having them with a man. I wasn't, so I told him. This brilliant professor scratches his head and says, "Oh, my ... I never dreamed ... but I thought you *did*."

You know what I do now? I masturbate right in front of the man so he'll know what I like. Words are inadequate, don't you think? It's better to demonstrate.

After the professor, I started dating this boy, Tom. He's my age. I had the idea of putting his hand on my clitoris when I didn't come, or when I wanted to come again.

Well, he didn't want to be bothered. He just wanted his orgasm, and then a little nap afterward. But I let him know I wouldn't sleep with him any more unless I got what *I* wanted out of it.

One of my very worst experiences was with a man in his forties. I met him at a wedding. We danced awhile and I asked him to my place. He positively *leered*. I thought, "Oh, boy! A dirty old man!"

I unzipped him the minute we got in the door and he came in my hand. Then we necked, got undressed and into bed, and had sex the usual way.

Afterward, he said, "Hey, I thought you came. But you want it again, don't you?"

I said, "Sure I do. I always do. Doesn't your wife?"

That blew his mind. He was pissed and he started to make excuses about needing a little more time. Then I showed him how I masturbate and his mind was blown *again*. He said, "Wow ... I never saw a *girl* do *that* before."

But the worst was when he was leaving. He offered me *money*. I screamed at him, "I'm no whore," and he left in a hurry. He belongs to *that* generation. I refuse to knock all older men, but ...

To be fair to older men, even some of the younger guys I know call me "whore," or "promiscuous," because I sleep with lots of different people. It isn't fair. I don't think of *men* as whores or promiscuous when they have a lot of women.

Fairness and equality, I think, are when men and women can just accept each other for what they are, individually. Maybe a long time from now you won't have to be writing about sexually aggressive women because they won't exist. We'll just have people. Men and women, some aggressive, some not, according to how they feel most comfortable.

I bet there will be a lot more like me in ten years.

Yes, I'm into bisexuality. Call it lesbianism if you want. I don't care. I do prefer men both physically and emotionally. Anyway, I have sex with both.

There's a difference between casual sex and a relationship. In a relationship, you share feelings, talk about problems, do things together. It isn't necessary to have a relationship to have sex.

At the moment, I have two relationships: Valerie for female sex and Bob for male sex.

Valerie and I talk for hours. We lie in bed nude hugging and kissing. Some people think you use giant dildoes, but we don't. We touch and rub and stroke and suck. With a woman I never feel rushed. Everything is easy and relaxed. That's the big difference, I think. With a woman, it's slow ... tender. With a man it's exciting.

Oh, and another thing. Women are more honest about it when they're not in the mood for screwing. Men are afraid to say they're too tired. Their masculinity is at stake. When I sense that a guy—Bob for example—is tired, I don't make an issue of it. I never think any less of a man if he can't get it up because he's exhausted or has something on his mind.

But I don't like it when a man falls asleep after sex. It's like he's saying, "Okay, I got what I wanted, now leave me alone." Women don't do that.

I spend more time with Bob than Valerie. Neither is jealous of the other as far as I know. They both see other people and I don't limit myself to them, either. I'm always up for something, or somebody, new.

I really get off on clothes. When I'm in the mood to meet somebody, I wear something that gets me looked at. It's like baiting the hook. I wear tight jeans mostly, usually with a shirt. But I freak on old Forties clothes. I have a blue flowered dress with padded shoulders and a low V neckline. It's jersey, very fluid and clingy, and just feeling it against my skin turns me on. Then I have a red satin mini dress. I wear it with five-inch platforms and I feel like the happy hooker. I love it.

A bar is the best place to meet men. I go with a girlfriend. If we see somebody we like, we go over and start talking. When the vibes are right and I decide I want to sleep with someone, I put my hand on his knee. Or, if it's not too obvious, I rest it in his lap. On his penis.

Back in my apartment, I'm usually the one who starts up. I can be playful about it—unbuttoning his shirt, giggling, tickling. Other times, I go down on him right away. I never met a guy who could resist it. If he doesn't do the same for me, I tell him it'd be better for him if he turns me on. Well . . . I don't use those words exactly, but something like it.

I'm not shy about asking for what I want. I have a vibrator, a present from a friend. If I think it would add to the situation, I get it out and show the guy how to use it. No, you don't just turn it on and stick it in. There's a certain angle. You want most of the vibration on your clitoris.

The most unlikely pickup I made was when a girlfriend and I were hitchhiking in Colorado. We found this cabin in the woods and we went to investigate. A guy came out. He was a very hairy, scary-looking person until you got up close, and then he was attractive in a peculiar way. He asked us inside and within fifteen minutes the three of us were doing it together. My mother would never recover if she knew about that one.

She [Ruth's mother] is about forty-five now. My parents go along as well as most but they weren't very physical with each other. I knew from the time I was little that my father had other women. She used to cry about it at night. I could hear her through the walls.

I think about sex a lot. I screw about four times a week, sometimes more. One thing I definitely am not, and that's a nymphomaniac. I don't even know if there is such a thing. Listen—I read this someplace and it makes sense: "A nymphomaniac is a term men apply to any woman who is their equal."

Ruth is another one of those confident, self-assured young women, who not only knows instinctively that what she does is right for herself, but also feels it is probably right for a lot of other women as well—and that many will soon be following her lead. ("I bet there will be a lot more like me in ten years," she says.)

She has observed that in her experience men often fall asleep after sex, while women do not. I wonder how many male—female relationships have foundered on this fact alone—how many women craving post-coital tenderness and affection were left seething with anger while their men, satiated, retreated into sleep. When a woman recognizes differences in post-coital behavior (obviously not all men fall asleep, nor are all women tender), she is in a better position to deal constructively with her needs rather than with outright or repressed resentment and hostility—which can only serve to undermine the good feelings within any relationship.

Helen

"I see marriage as a trap."

Helen, twenty-four, is a big-boned woman with long, very curly—almost frizzy—dark brown hair, heavy eyebrows, and a generous mouth painted crimson to match her long, carefully manicured nails. Certainly not pretty, but with a commanding presence, she sits calmly, seemingly very much at ease with the prospect of our talk.

She lives with her current lover and works as a secretary. The oldest of three children, her own apartment is half an hour away from her parents' home, which she visits about once a month, "partly out of love, partly out of duty."

My mother taught me the good girl bit, but it didn't take, if you know what I mean. She always said, "Save sex for the man you marry, otherwise no one respects you."

She doesn't like the way I live ... doesn't know what to make of it. My mother and father both know that I'm living with Stu. Not that I ever *told* them. But Stu's always around, and it's a one-bedroom apartment, and he's obviously not just a roommate. I've explained how I feel about him, and they see him as a son-in-law—a prospective son-in-law—although we're definitely not planning a wedding. Not now.

My first sex was at seventeen, and, no, I wasn't aggressive then. For a long time, this boy was after me to do it and finally I did. I liked fucking right away. It felt good. I didn't feel guilty about it because the boy stayed with me—it wasn't a matter of scoring and then cutting out on me.

I became sexually aggressive with my second boyfriend. I was in my last year of high school. We were with each other three years. We grew up together. We were attracted to one another physically at first. That's always first. Once you get the sex over, you can communicate. Once you get over being inhibited, you have a better understanding of what's happening. You can talk about anything. I asked questions, we discussed positions, how it felt when we did certain things to each other. You have to be able to talk about it; after that, actions speak louder than words.

My definition of a sexually aggressive woman is the woman who sees somebody she wants and then pursues him. I do that now. If I meet someone and he appeals to me, I pursue. Verbally, or with my eyes. I give off warm feelings. Vibrations. It's true, you know. If you really concentrate, you can get someone's attention.

I do it everywhere. Walking down the street, in clubs, at parties. I don't go to bars that often.

I like a tall, slim, dark-haired man best. A couple of weeks ago, in the lobby of a bank, I saw a knock-out man. I stared at him and then I went over and we talked. He asked me what I was doing after work and I told him I'd like to be with him.

He was staying at a hotel, so we met in the lobby, had a drink, then went upstairs to the room. We sat around talking. A couple of his friends dropped in. We drank some more and then we all went out for something to eat. The sex came later.

I'm aggressive enough to draw a man to me by staring and concentrating, but once in a while I let the guy get the feeling that *he's* doing the pursuing. I mean, I'll look at him, so he'll know I'm interested, but he'll do the actual physical thing of walking over to talk. He can have his manhood that way.

In bed, I'm aggressive too. If I'm not satisfied, I'll talk about it afterward. I'll deflate a man's ego if it takes that to let him know I'm not satisfied. If he goes down on me I almost always come. So I tell him that's what I want him to do. I think I should be satisfied—it shouldn't be just one way, all for him.

I do a lot with my mouth. Go up and down a guy's body with my tongue. But only if I'm excited. I can't produce if I'm not excited enough. When I go down and lick and suck his penis he really digs it. Any guy. That seems to be the ultimate for a man.

For me, I like oral sex first, and then I tell him when I'm ready for his penis inside my vagina. It's not barking commands or giving orders, though. It's whispering, just loud enough for him to hear.

With Stu, we sometimes make straight love first and then have oral sex later. But when I first knew him he wouldn't lick my pussy. He didn't think it was disgusting or anything like that. But he didn't feel the time was right. He said it's just about as far as a person can go in bed, and that it was like a treat and he wanted to save it until he really cared. I told him I didn't feel it should be saved.

I was faithful to Stu for about a year and then he started running around and it blew my mind. He was taking me for granted and I just decided that I was young and attractive and there were other men that I could be interested in. So now I see other guys, but Stu and I are still together. I'm a woman with feelings, just like he's a man with feelings, and so we have this very loose arrangement. But I'm his woman at home and I feel that I have first priority.

I feel that any relationship should be equal. If I'm going to be fully dedicated to a guy, I want the same. But there's no way I can get enough if he's out screwing around. So I go out and screw around, too.

If I'm in the mood to make love and he's there, we make love. If I'm out and I see someone who appeals to me, it'll go on from there. Whatever happens, happens.

I've had about ten men but Stu is my best lover because he likes to experiment and try new positions. The first time I had anal sex was with him. Sometimes we don't wait to go to bed to screw. We might be eating breakfast, or sitting on the couch, and next thing I know, he's licking my pussy. He's exciting and he has a lot on the ball upstairs.

I like sex four or five times a week and I ask for more if I need it. If one orgasm isn't enough for me, I give him time to relax. We rap a while. I help him rest his mind while his body's resting. Half an hour's usually enough, and then I go down on him and we start off again.

I feel a woman's got to have a positive head. If you feel insecure or have an inferiority complex, it shows. What turns me on to a person and makes me hang in there with a person is learning. I ask a lot of questions and the man I'm with has to have other kinds of knowledge than I do because if he can't teach me anything, I don't want him. If he doesn't know what's happening in the world then for me it's just a one-night affair. I may find him physically attractive, but after one night the hell with it, no matter how good the sex is.

I also think the woman is more powerful than the man. I'm talking in generalities now, but for the most part a woman has a choice, a man doesn't. If the woman doesn't want sex, there's nothing the man can do. I mean, a woman can always arouse a man, but a man can't arouse a woman if her head isn't on sex.

Some people say a man uses a woman's body. I don't feel that way. A lot of times a woman will use a man's body, because it takes more for a woman to be satisfied. A man's ego is involved, so he has to go along with it. In the end, his body may be *over*used, while a woman is just getting fulfilled.

I've never told my boyfriend about my other men because it's unnecessary. I've been very fair with him and I've been faithful in my head even though I've slept with others.

Living with him is almost like a marriage. Sometimes I have to be with someone else in order to keep our relationship on an even keel. I have a tendency to nag, and he hassles me a lot. So I go out and have a good time to get away from all that.

Right now I'm not on the Pill and I don't have an I.U.D. I'm not using anything because sometimes I think about having a child. But I don't want to get married. It scares me. Stu wants to get married. He wanted to even before we started living together, but I told him, "No, I'll live with you but it won't be a marriage on paper." I see marriage as a trap.

If I do get married, it won't be planned. I'll have to do it without thinking too much about it. It will be an impulsive thing, otherwise I'll back out.

I have a girlfriend, and before she and her husband were married they lived together for a year and everything was beautiful. Then they got married and in three months they were separated.

One thing I know. I need a relationship. I think I'm typical of my generation. To live a life of continuous affairs is a big blank. You get nothing from it. But what's the alternative?

I think a man has a fear of responsibility and marriage spells responsibility and obligation. He becomes responsible for you and you become dependent, more or less, and if you don't want to work, you really don't have to, and then you're nowhere. The marriage license ... it's just a piece of paper but it causes trouble. Now I could be wrong, but that's how I feel.

I know I could take care of a child by myself. Stu wants a child, too. I'm not saying I wouldn't marry him eventually, after the child was born. But I would just like to try it this way ... keep things the way they are.

The fact that I'm capable of earning my own living, that I know where my head is at, even though it might not be at the same place five years from now—those are the most important things. I do want to belong to someone. I'm just not ready yet for the big commitment.

It would be difficult to find a better example of the dilemma confronting so many sexually aggressive women than that described by Helen. She craves a close emotional tie, and all but invites the birth of a child, yet she balks at the prospect of surrendering freedom and independence.

"To live a life of continuous affairs is a big blank," she says. "You get nothing from it." Marriage, however, is a trap in which she feels she will lose her identity. She can more easily contemplate the responsibility of being a mother than the loss of self connected (in her mind, at least) with being a wife.

Very possibly, marriage to a man like Stu would be untenable for Helen. His sexual and cultural perspectives are far more traditional than hers. (He was reluctant to engage in oral sex; he wanted to marry Helen even before they moved in together.)

Helen, like many of these young women, is in the process of synthesizing her varied experiences. Hopefully when she is further along in the process she will be better able to reconcile her conflicting needs.

Cathy

"I feel important to be fucking a man who's famous all around the world."

Cathy, eighteen, is a truly beautiful young woman. Her long silky hair is the color of ripe wheat, her teeth are a dazzling white, her skin a perfect, pale, pale peach. Except for her breasts, which are large in proportion to the rest of her, her figure is model-slim, with legs that seem to go on forever. Her voice is childishly high. In fact, there is much about Cathy that is childishly young for eighteen.

She is a groupie. Her man is a rock superstar of such magnitude that even people who care little about such things are familiar with his name. Cathy has been part of his entourage for six months now.

My parents hate me. They won't talk to me. But I don't care. I worked as a waitress and saved my money until I had enough to live on for a while. Then I just took off and started following X's group around the country.

There are always a lot of really beautiful girls around, so you have to be persistent. I went to every performance in every town and after two months he finally noticed me.

His manager just came up and said, "X wants to

meet you." I nearly fainted. We had dinner, then we went to bed.

I was a virgin and he was a little surprised about that, but he was nice. He really helped me understand what it was all about. I had been to a doctor to have my hymen stretched, so that part was okay. And I knew from talking to my girlfriends that I wouldn't enjoy it the first time. Now it's getting better.

The boys I knew in school ... they're dumb. Just kids. This life I have now is what I always wanted. It's exciting. It's kicks. It's a wonderful feeling that X digs *me*. I know it won't last forever, but while it does ... well, I'm loving every single minute. I feel important to be fucking a man who's famous all around the world.

Sometimes he gets philosophical. Once he said to me, "A guy in my business could screw himself to death. He's pussy-whipped. He could turn into a mechanical man." I didn't feel put down. After all, he chose *me*.

He's teaching me a lot. I'm learning all the tricks. Sucking him off. The whole bit. He showed me just how he likes it. I put my mouth way over his penis; I get it in as far as it will go. He just lays there and groans and that turns me on. I can make X moan and groan and beg for more!

What he does to me is, he starts with my hair. He loves it because it's long and naturally blonde. He plays with it, runs his fingers through it. He holds me. He kisses me all over. Just the other night, for the first time, he licked my clitoris. I never knew anything about the different parts of my body, even what a clitoris was.

He says when I'm more experienced and when I can handle it up here—in my head—he'll bring in another woman. It's okay with me.

He gave me some books to read. Sex books that tell different ways to do it. So I'm learning fast. I know what it's all about.

I didn't want to be broken in by some guy in high school or the local gas-station guy. I wanted somebody better. Well, look at me. I mean, I know I'm beautiful and I deserve better than some clunky kid.

I clip all the articles in the papers and magazines about X. I know all his records, all his tunes by heart. I love the conversation. Being an insider. Hearing all the inside gossip. Listening to the guys rap. I smoke a little grass with the guys and I like it fine. Somebody—not X—tried to turn me on to other stuff, but I won't get hung up on *that*. I'm smart enough to know what happens.

I picked X because he's famous and rich and because of the way he looks. He's very handsome to me. Very sexy. Getting to know someone like him is fantastic. I have a lot of feelings for him, even though he keeps warning me it—our thing—will be over soon. I know I can't expect too much.

My parents? They were very strict. Once they caught me playing around with the little boy next door. I guess we were about six. We were just showing each other how we looked. I had my dress up, showing him my vagina—my "crack" I called it—and he was showing me his little peepee. All kids do it. I know that now. But my mother was mean about it. She punished me as though I'd committed a terrible crime.

I turned her off more and more as I grew up. I pretended to listen to her, but I didn't really. I acted like a good girl, the way she wanted me to act, just to keep from being punished. The punishment would be staying in my room, or getting a spanking, or not being allowed to go to the beach. That was the worst—having to stay home with my grandmother on beautiful summer days.

Now I guess I'm punishing her. Getting even with them. My Dad, too. They sent me to a psychiatrist once because they thought I wasn't acting right, and he explained I was trying to get back at them for what they did to me.

I was an only child and I didn't have many girlfriends, and the ones I did have ... well, we didn't talk much about boys or sex. So I think I've really changed a lot and come a long way.

School was a drag. Living at home was a drag. One day when I was still in high school I picked up this magazine and read about girls who were groupies. "That's what I want," I thought. "That's exactly what I want to do."

So I got myself a job as a waitress on the weekends and after school, and saved my money; in six months I had a few hundred dollars.

Then I read that X was going to be doing a show in Chicago—which is about fifty miles away from my home—and I just got on a bus and that was that. I left a note and told them not to bother to try and find me.

A couple of months later I telephoned. I wanted them to know I was okay. My mother broke down and cried and begged me to come home, but I said, "No, I like my life. This is it." I have a feeling when I'm older I'll be able to go and see them, but I'll never live with them again.

After I started sleeping with X, I went out with a guy my age. He was a groupie-groupie. A guy who follows the groupies who follow the musicians. I picked him up in the audience at one of X's concerts. I slept with him and it was awful. He didn't know one part from another. A big dumb kid, nice-looking. Who needs it?

Money is no problem now. I can always pick up an odd job here and there. X pays for some of my meals and buys me things sometimes, but I wouldn't, you know, actually take *money* from him. He'd give it to me if I asked, but that's not why I'm doing this thing.

The question—the big question—is what's going to happen to me when X decides it's all over. I don't know. I really don't. I guess I'll get a full-time job and just see what happens. But anyway, I'm not worried yet. There's a black girl hanging around a lot now and I can tell he thinks she's something, but I'm not worried yet.

X has a very nice secretary, and she talks to me sometimes, about my future and things like that. I think she's trying to prepare me for being dumped. She said she'd help me find a job if I ever need one. She says she thinks I ought to see a shrink ... that I have problems. I don't know.

Cathy really does need therapy. She is caught up in the idea of being sexually aggressive and revels in the "freedom" of her new life (although I do not see her as being free at all; X, obviously, has almost total power over her). But much of what she says and does is motivated not so much by the need to express herself, as it is by revenge against unsympathetic parents.

Unlike the others, she demonstrates truly destructive behavior and refuses to consider seriously the pitfalls that lie ahead. She is still very young, of course, but unless she gets professional help or faces her neurotic behavior herself, as a prelude to change, her future looks disastrous.

Sarah

"I'm more aware of how a woman's body functions [and so] I feel surer of myself with women."

Sarah has a quick, sharp mind and her face is wonderfully expressive: her eyes beam with enthusiasm and squint in concentration; sardonic smiles alternate with grimaces of disgust.

She wears large, pink-tinted aviator glasses, jeans, and a sweatshirt. Her skin is somewhat blotchy. Little wisps of hair escape from the bun she has fastened—none too expertly—with a rubber band atop her head. She gives the impression of being much too busy to bother with the niceties of good grooming.

She dropped out of college for two years but is back now, finishing her last semester. She sees her parents occasionally and describes her childhood as "comfortable." She is twenty-four.

I think it's funny that you want women to come in and talk about being sexually aggressive. I don't think about it. As an anthropology major, I understand what you're after. You want to know if *we're* doing it differently. My age group. Some of us are. I am.

I don't really think men and women play

active/passive roles any more. At least I don't know anyone who does. If I feel like having sex, I make a pass.

I've had some relationships with women, and I've found that it really doesn't matter very much if you're with a male or a female. It's a human being you're relating to. With either a man or a woman, if I want to be sexually aggressive, I can say, "Let's turn on some music, have a couple of drinks and go to bed."

If the other person wants to adopt some kind of role, it's their prerogative. I don't. I think fondling is just the result of affection. You like someone . . . you kiss and hug and hold hands and eventually it leads to something more passionate. Then you get undressed and go to bed.

I don't have a particular behavior pattern when I feel like having sex. It depends on the situation and the person.

I meet people through friends, through school. I never slept with anyone I picked up at a bar. I get very negative feelings about that—whether it's a gay bar or a bar for heterosexual people, it still seems like a meat rack to me. It's offensive.

To date, I've had four men and four women.

I had a very good sexual relationship with one guy. But he was young and it was difficult for him to handle his feelings about my aggressiveness. I would sit with him on the couch, nibble his ear, push him down, start kissing him. I didn't wait for him. It was okay for a while, but then his insecurity took over. I think it's cultural conditioning. He thought he was supposed to make most of the passes and that I was supposed to be reluctant at first and then give in to him. At least that's the way it seemed to me.

He never said no to me when I wanted sex. And he was never impotent. But I just knew he felt uncomfortable when I made the first move. The sex was good, but at the same time, he felt, "I'm a man, and this is not proper behavior for a man."

The funny thing about it was that I picked up on his fantasies and I felt we were getting into something very affectionate—*and* physical. He never had to perform. If he felt like just relaxing, it was okay with me. I never forced him. We could just sit, hold each other, and talk. It was the first time he ever had a thing like that with a woman.

It seems that often when a couple aren't very much in love—we weren't because it didn't last long enough—they tend to play sexual roles. They don't let their defenses down because they don't feel free with each other. When a relationship lasts a long time, or the couple are married, they can really *be themselves* together.

In sex, I like to be stroked all over, and some men aren't into doing that. I'm not blunt, but I'll show what I want. If you have to say, "I really would like it if you'd rub my back," you've missed the boat. If you've made a good choice, the person you're with will be aware enough and sensitive enough to pick up on what you want.

If a man puts his arm around me and strokes my neck and I say, "Oh, that feels good," I'm letting him know that I like to be touched that way. If I do it to him and he says, "Oh, that feels good," then I know what he likes.

It's experimenting. I like to squeeze people, but if I squeeze someone under the arms and they say, "That's ticklish," or "It hurts," then I understand they don't enjoy that.

No, I wouldn't ask anyone for oral sex, but most men I've slept with volunteer sooner or later. If I have to ask, it's not enjoyable. It's stiff.

I usually use the clinical term. Fellatio. I've never done that to a guy. It's more often that a man will perform cunnilingus on me.

Nobody's forcing anybody else to have sex, so it should be easygoing, not a strain, not a struggle. It should be mutually relaxing. But the first time can be difficult. You're exploring, finding out what the other person likes, what you like. It's delicate, but getting to know someone and how they respond and what they like—that's half the enjoyment.

With women I find myself very aggressive. Maybe because I'm with my own kind, and I'm more aware of how a woman's body functions. I feel sure of myself.

With men, I go slower at first. I don't want to blow anybody's mind in one session, so I approach with subtlety. I know that men have penises and so forth, but I'm not a man, I don't know what it feels like to *be* a man, or what a man's orgasm is like or what turns him on and makes him feel good. Maybe as I get more experience with men, I'll be just as aggressive as I am with women. Maybe I go slower with men now because of that other relationship I told you about—the one that just fizzled.

One of the problems with bisexuality is that it's very in fashion with college women now. I hear a woman say, "I'm bisexual," parading it. I resent that kind of talk; if you're really bisexual you don't have to shout about it. You do it.

I think it would be nice some day if both men and women are free to express affection or love toward either sex. It's very difficult now—because of all the things you learn while you're growing up and because of the society we live in.

I don't think bisexuality is a result of the woman's movement. I think it has more to do with the men. They don't appear as masculine and this has affected women. A lot of the rock stars act and look very feminine and college men dress unisex. You sleep with a man who looks like a woman, and the next step is to sleep with a woman.

I was rejected by a woman once at a party. I was eighteen and it was in a small town. Everybody was fooling around. This woman and I were dancing together and she said, "Let's go upstairs." We just necked a little and then she got very hostile when I began unbuttoning her blouse. It was total disaster. She had taken me to be a female-role lesbian, which I'm not. I'm just me.

I feel it's great if I can have good relationships with both sexes. The main thing about relating bisexually is it helps me relate more freely to men. I feel more positive about myself when I understand that women can define themselves and not be just *things* defined by men. I can be a person, responsive, affectionate, and aggressive with men and women. If I feel like jumping on top of a guy, then I can do it. I don't feel embarrassed. I realize it may be difficult for him, but seeing him as a human being, like myself, helps me overcome it.

I don't hesitate to call a guy. I'll say, "How've you been, let's get together or come over for dinner." I do the same with women. I don't feel I have to wait for my women friends to ask me out, so why should I feel that way with the men I like? They're people.

Now I try not to get involved with guys that are hung up on male roles and who want me to wait around for them to make the first move. I can't be bothered. I want to relate to *people*.

Sexual fidelity ... there are degrees of it. It has to be decided on and agreed between the two people. You determine how you want it to be. I've been with men where we didn't choose fidelity and if we slept with other people, it was okay in terms of our arrangement. Other times, it was understood that there would be no outside sex, and if we were unfaithful, it hurt our relationship.

Because I tend to be aggressive, I feel I'm helping the men I sleep with to grow. A man may not be able to handle it in the long run and the relationship might dissolve—like that other one—but he's learned something and I've helped him.

I feel that a lot of men are very *unliberated*, as much as a lot of women, only in different ways. How much better off we'd all be if we could just be free enough to follow our natural inclinations.

I'm bisexual, but maybe somebody I'll place all my stock in men. It's culturally more rewarding because you can get married. Lesbians usually don't. I don't want to give in to the culture but I recognize the possibility that at some point in my life I might.

Sarah, in a single statement, denies the entire patriarchal tradition in Western culture when she says, "I don't think men and women play active/passive roles anymore. At least I don't know anyone who does." The statement assumes the quality of wishful thinking later on when she contradicts herself in describing a short affair with a young man who had difficulty accepting her aggressiveness. But she is an idealist who is trying, in the best way she knows, to redefine the conventional male–female relationship. If major cultural changes are to be made, I believe they will be made mainly by women like Sarah.

She views bisexuality as a pleasurable way of expressing her own sexuality, and also as an ultimate good for the culture; through it, men and women will arrive at a more human and basic understanding of one another.

She is aware that acting against the culture is not easy, and she fears she will capitulate at some later stage in her life. There is always the possibility, though, that she and others like her will change the society in such a way that heterosexual marriage can be reconciled with having relationships with members of one's own sex.

Margaret

"I decided that, I ... an ex-nun ... would now ... take the next step and get laid."

Margaret, thirty, is an ex-nun; it isn't difficult to imagine her in a habit instead of the light blue shirt-waist dress she wore when we met. Everything about her is soft and rather quiet: her voice, her light brown hair, her eyes, and her hands, which remained folded in her lap for most of the interview.

Margaret works as a secretary now. She has her own apartment, although her parents and her married brothers and sisters (there are five of them) live nearby in the same section of the city.

Many Catholic girls start wanting to be nuns when they're six or seven. I did. I never thought of being anything else. When I think about my childhood, it was all church and school and praying to God and Jesus and the Virgin. I don't think I ever had fun. I was a very serious ... pious ... little girl.

I didn't know anything about boys. My two brothers were strangers to me. I went to an all-girls' school. The only dates I had before I went into the convent were for my junior and senior proms, and a girlfriend arranged them. I was very nervous both times.

Of course there was no such thing as sex for me in high school. I never kissed anyone. I never masturbated until I left the convent. It never occurred to me.

Please don't laugh at this. My first sexual feelings came from reading some James Bond books. My mother brought them when she visited me at the convent. I was intrigued by certain passages. I felt vaguely excited when I read them. I would go back to them over and over.

I never thought of myself as a woman who could be attractive to men. Not even when the curate where I was teaching started to talk to me in the halls—it was only small talk, after all—but he sent me flowers on Christmas.

When he left my parish to go to South America, he called long distance from the airport. We wrote regularly until last year, and in one of his letters, he said, "It's a shame we didn't get to know each other better." Now I realize that he must have liked me as a woman. He was the first; I was twenty-six and didn't see his interest as anything but pure friendliness.

I spent ten years in the convent. I went in at eighteen and came out at twenty-eight. I left because I was unhappy, depressed, tired all the time. I had a sense of tightening up. I was living on tranquilizers, and I kept thinking to myself, "This is ridiculous; why do I need to relax more? I have no energy as it is."

I thought a change would help, so I asked to be transferred to another mission. When I got there I felt even worse. My new superior was unyielding, unbending, and mean. She only added to my misery.

I have an uncle who is a Christian Brother and a guidance counselor, and one day when he visited me he said, "I hate to think of what will happen to you if you don't get out of here, Margaret. This is not for you."

Still . . . the idea of wanting to be a nun and to teach was strong. I'm stubborn and it was the only way of life I knew, so it took me three more months to face the fact that it wasn't my superior, it wasn't the conditions of the convent, it was *me*. Other people could be happy nuns, but not Margaret.

The truth drove me into a panic. I stopped functioning . . . I stayed in bed and couldn't teach. I knew I had to leave so I called my mother, made all the arrangements, and went home.

Within two weeks I had a job with an insurance company. I was out in the world for the first time in my life, feeling confused and unprotected. I had so much to learn.

I was suddenly very interested in men. There were lots of men in the office. All ages, shapes, and sizes. I'd never seen so many in one place. I was much too shy to goof with them the way the other girls did.

The first man I ever really noticed—in my whole life—was a junior executive, very junior. He wore glasses, was probably about my age, didn't seem very bright. But he *talked to me*. He would stop at my desk and ask how I liked the job, did I have a nice weekend. But he never asked me out.

Well . . . no wonder. I weighed about one eighty. I

knew if I wanted to date, I'd have to lose weight. I went on a diet and lost fifty pounds of baby fat. Blubber. I practiced with makeup and hairstyles. I bought some new clothes. I was like a teen-ager getting in shape for life.

One night I took myself—the "new me"—to an Irish club and met a man. I can't remember his name. We went to a movie and he told me I was stiff and uptight, even just to talk to. He didn't try to kiss me, and I had wanted him to, so much. All through the movie I had had a warm, excited, breathless feeling sitting next to him.

I remember going to the library at about this time and borrowing all the sex books on the shelf. Don't forget, I knew about as much as ... as a five-year-old.

I was amazed at what I read in some of those books. Yes, I knew how men and women conceived babies, but the rest—the descriptions of weird positions, cunnilingus, fellatio, anal penetration—why would anyone want to do those things? They weren't necessary for making babies. Kissing was one thing. Putting a penis in your mouth! At that time, the idea was just ... ugh!

I thought a lot about what I'd read. And the longer I thought, the less strange and wrong those things seemed. Finally, I began to imagine how it would feel doing them. Having them done to me.

Around that time, I heard about a group of ex-priests and nuns who met once a week, and I decided to join them. We talked, we shared experiences. It was my whole social life for a while.

I felt drawn to one of the ex-priests, a tall, graying

man, about forty, with the most incredible blue eyes. Not handsome but ... "magnetic" is the word. I found myself daydreaming about him. My feelings for him were sexual. In fact I had fantasies of doing the things I had read about—with him.

But in my head, sex and marriage went together. You couldn't—or you *shouldn't*—have one without the other. So I had to make myself believe I was in love with him. Otherwise, my feelings would have been wrong. I didn't come to this conclusion in a logical step one, step two, step three way of course. But now I can see how my mind was operating.

I'd been watching the girls in my office—the way some of them went after the men they liked, how they got noticed. I applied their techniques with Tom, the ex-priest. At the meetings, I stayed close to him, made sure I sat next to him, touched his arm, looked straight into his eyes when he talked. It worked. He asked me out.

It's hard to describe, but it was like the world opened to me that night. He kissed me. His tongue in my mouth was ... shivery ... thrilling. It was like someone else was living in my body and this person—a new Margaret—took over. It was she who guided Tom's hand to my breast, unbuttoned my blouse.

But the old Margaret came back when he slid his hand under the elastic of my panties. I pulled away. I laughed a little. Apologized. "I can't do it. I still feel it's wrong so I just can't ... I'm sorry." I was embarrassed. My words embarrassed me. My feelings embarrassed me. My virginity embarrassed me. There was a word I'd heard at the office, "cock-teaser." Was that me?

But he didn't use that word and he wasn't angry. He smiled and shrugged and said, "When you're ready, call me."

This is the most embarrassing part. I let it all out then. I told him I loved him, I wanted to marry him, I'd sleep with him when we were married. I feel myself blushing whenever I think about it.

He was kind, though. He said, "Look, Margaret, I'm flattered that you think you're in love with me, but you're like a child. You were a *nun*, for God's sake, until a year ago. You don't know what the world's all about. Or me. Especially me. Go home and think about it."

I couldn't sleep that night. I remembered his tongue and his hands and the way he smelled and the feeling of falling, falling off into space. I put my hand down between my legs and squeezed my thighs together and it felt like ... nothing. There was an ache. Yes, it was an ache—to be held, and stroked, and filled. I was empty, and I felt I'd die if I didn't get filled.

I made a conscious decision. I decided that I, Margaret, a good Catholic girl who became a nun at eighteen and an ex-nun at twenty-eight, would now, at twenty-nine, take the next step and get laid. I'd never used that term before, but it popped into my head then, and it made me happy to think about it. "Getting laid" by an ex-priest who would not marry me and did not love me. I would do this thing for one reason only. The ache was too strong to resist.

I called him the next morning and he told me to come to his place that evening.

On the way over, I suddenly thought, "What about contraceptives! I might have a *baby!*" I burst in the door with "Tom, Tom, what about birth control?" He opened a drawer and brought out a funny-looking rubbery little rolled-up thing. The first condom I'd ever seen.

We sat down, had a drink, listened to rock music. I would have liked softer, more romantic music. "Some Enchanted Evening" with violins. But . . .

It's hard to describe how it feels to see a nude man for the first time. Patches of hair . . . muscles . . . the penis. I thought it would be much bigger. It was a floppy little worm at first. Then, as I watched, it got straighter and stiffer. It . . . *grew.*

He did my whole body. He used his hands and his tongue. I moaned . . . I heard myself moaning and I remember wondering if other women moaned, too.

He put his finger in my vagina. It was wet and I worried that he might not like it to be wet and slimy.

Then, that moment when his penis slipped inside. Who can say what it's like? Relief, satisfaction. Being hungry and not eating for weeks, and then the first taste of food. That's as close as I can come to it.

I didn't have an orgasm with Tom. I didn't have an orgasm with John, the second man I slept with. I've *never* had an orgasm with a man. I only come when I masturbate. Funny. I feel guilty about that . . . the masturbating, and not coming with a man.

I don't feel conscious guilt about the rest. I love being touched and kissed and held. I love being naked and playing with a man. Taking baths together. Tickling.

I'm finally able to put a penis in my mouth. It wasn't easy. I thought it might smell and I was afraid it would suddenly ... you know, "explode" ... in my mouth. I could never do that, swallow semen. But then again, maybe I could. I didn't think I could lick and suck and kiss a penis, either.

I still see Tom. He's upset when I don't have orgasms, so sometimes I pretend. It occurs to me that men have fragile egos when it comes to sex. They don't understand that you might enjoy it even if you don't come.

It seems like five thousand years ago that I felt sex and marriage *had* to go together. I want to get married and I will and when I do, I'll be faithful. But sex is important and I think it would be bad, wrong, to marry someone you hadn't slept with.

Other girls who're my age and who've been doing this sort of thing since they were eighteen or twenty—they have years of experience. I've only been around for two years. I still don't know how to flirt in a bar and just ... get things going. I hear girls say, "I met him and I decided he was the one I wanted, and I got him." I *think* that way but I'm still unsure about how to do it.

But, well ... I've come a long, long way in a short time. So, maybe next year ...

Margaret, because of her strict Catholic upbringing and the long years spent in the convent, is emo-

tionally and sexually behind the other young singles. But she has come a long way in a relatively short time and although she expresses a desire for a fairly conventional life—one man, marriage, and children—I can't help but wonder whether even these goals might not be modified within the next year or so.

(For example, she doesn't say anything about wanting bisexual experiences—but up until recently, neither did she have a conscious need for heterosexual experiences.)

Margaret is changing faster and more drastically than any of the other young singles I talked with. She certainly pursued her first lover most aggressively in the face of all but overwhelming fear and inexperience. Where she will finally end up on the scale of aggressiveness is anybody's guess.

Pamela

"I can have sex two times a day with two different men."

Pamela, twenty-six, conveys an exotic, gypsyish quality: her wild black hair tumbles down her back in ringlets, her dark eyes flash as she talks, and though her usual expression is serious and intense, her grin, when it breaks through, is decidedly roguish.

She works as a waitress and is presently living communally with eight other people in a house not far from the large Eastern university from which she graduated.

Her family is religious and as a child she went with them to a Fundamentalist Presbyterian church, where, Sunday after Sunday, she heard the pleasures of the body denounced as evil.

I wanted sex from the time I was twelve, and thinking back, it seems incredible that I was able to hold out until twenty-one. Poor kid I was then. My parents and the church telling me sex was a sin; my body and my friends telling me, "Do it, it's okay, you'll like it."

I fantasized and masturbated for *years*. It was such a relief when it finally happened and I actually slept with someone.

For me, becoming sexually aggressive wasn't a gradual process at all. I was aggressive from the beginning. I loved it from the first. It was suddenly like all the old things I'd been taught in church and at home, and ... just in general, by society ... they all became meaningless.

I don't mean to put down my parents or the church. I understand them. Sex is great, although maybe they don't know it or admit it. But even I know it's only part of life and not life itself. It's just that when you hold it up there like some precious diamond, you get a distorted view. You see it as something more, or less, or different than it really is.

I have to masturbate to orgasm, or have the man masturbate me. I don't usually come otherwise, so I ask the guy to use his hand on me. I can also come if we're doing 69. I have to be pretty high on grass or wine or something to come during straight intercourse. When I do come, I don't want sex again for a while. I mean I can't come more than once, and that's the way I am, so it's fine with me.

I've had some pretty good lovers. I've slept with about twenty-five men, and almost all of them I'd define as being "good." I feel okay about telling men what I want. I'll ask a guy to suck my nipples or lick my vagina. I also like to have my ears sucked. Silly, no? Anyway, it turns me on. Most of the men I've slept with were people I knew pretty well, and maybe that's why I can ask for what I want. I don't feel as free with a very business type of guy, or people that I've just met.

I was out West recently and I had my first trio experience. My girlfriend and I were just walking down the street and this nice, long-haired type picked us up. We started talking and we all liked each other right away. There were just very pleasant nice vibrations all around. So I said, "Why don't we all make it together," and we did. The man made love to my friend and me, then we made love to him. There wasn't too much happening between me and my friend, though. Kissing and hugging and licking, yes, but nothing vaginal.

I think I'm up for bisexuality on the basis of that one experience. I'm sorry my friend and I didn't get into it more. I've known her for five years. I wouldn't go out and pick up just any woman for sex.

It feels good to have a man inside you. A woman would be something different, but I don't think she could take the place of a man. Not for me.

I lived with a man for three years and we had sex almost every single night. When you get used to that, and then you go without it for a while, it gets to be actually physically painful.

Once there was this guy in the commune. I'd known him for about two months and I really wanted to fuck him. I decided one night to get undressed and fling my titties at him. We all had rooms of our own, so I knocked on his door, went in, looked at him for a few minutes—neither of us said anything—and then I just took my clothes off. I teased him then, touched his prick, under his jeans. He took me in his arms and was very ... masculine. To me that means gentle caressing and touching ... holding me ... making me feel comfortable and wanted.

I used to do this with some of the men in the commune; or I might initiate something at a party. But I never go to bars.

I like to go to bed with a man who is fairly intelligent and what I call respectable. By that I don't mean an uptight business type, but, you know, someone *into* something. A student, maybe, or a guy who's doing things with his hands, into making things. I don't like drifters or guys who are strung out.

Physically, my preference is a tall, slender man. I like a guy with a long penis and whose balls hang like a tall, proud horse. I can sense if a man is built like that even before I see him nude. I don't like beefy men, muscle men. I'm tall and muscular—for a woman—so you might think I'd prefer a bigger man, but I don't.

A lot of sexual things that are supposed to be freaky don't freak me out at all. I think I'd enjoy them. I'd like to get into a set that swings. But I don't know where to go. A good solid foursome would be great, and I'd also dig doing it with two guys. But not too many of the people I know are up for that. You have to find them through those swingers magazines.

I think about my parents and their sexual relationship. My mother comes off like she's old-fashioned and prudish, but when I got older she told me she slept with my father before they were married. I think that's really neat, and I liked her a lot better after she told me. I don't think she ever cheated on him. They never, never brought me up to feel masturbation was bad, and that's surprising, considering how religious she is and all.

I said before that I only have one orgasm. I forgot to say that two hours later I'm usually feeling horny again. I can have sex two times a day with two different men. It happened once when I went to my girlfriend's apartment and a bisexual guy was there. He was more gay than straight. He told me he hadn't had a woman in about two years. We got high on grass and I asked him—I came right out and said—"You'd really like to make love with me, right?" And he said yes, so we did. Then that night I went to bed with the guy I was going with at the time.

Lately some of my friends from school who got married at twenty-one are getting divorced at twenty-six or twenty-seven. Something's wrong. Some of them are splitting up because of adultery—what a corny, old-fashioned word. Because one went out and cheated on the other. It's just absurd. What a ridiculous reason to break up a relationship. Marriage rules have got to change.

I want love and tenderness, too. A warm, human relationship. I'd like to have a family. I'd like a husband, but he has to be the kind of man who would understand that I might want to go out and ball someone else occasionally. He would be my main man but every once in a while, I'd have something going with another guy.

I really want kids. I don't think it's right to bring a child into the kind of world we live in without having the security of a father. I think a family is definitely important. So, like I said, I want to get married, even though one part of me thinks it stinks. I'm out there searching like everybody else.

But I don't know if I'll find anyone who'll accept

me on my own terms. All men are chauvinists, I don't care how liberated they think they are. They just have to learn that some women are into a new thing.

Let me give you an example. The guy I go with thinks he's for women's liberation. He is, in a way. In a restaurant, I pay for my own food. Fine. I want it that way. But *he* wants to order for me, because that's "correct and proper." I can be as correct and proper as anyone, but sometimes it gets me angry. If I'm paying for it then it's up to *me* to decide whether he should order or not.

This guy, the one I see now, is also living in the commune. There are eight of us and we have it worked out so that we each have our own opposite-sex partner and we're absolutely faithful within the commune. In the beginning, we tried being free, sleeping with anyone who was living there in the house. But it just didn't work out. Now we find that respecting each other's sexual privacy makes for better vibrations. Outside, that's different. Each one of the four women has other men at times.

I find life warm and loving and good. I work. I smoke a little grass on weekends. Not a lot; I don't overdo it. My main problem is deciding on a career. I do waitressing just to earn money, but I'd really like to get into nursing or some other work where I can feel I'm giving to people who need it.

I can remember back when I was little and in church. The minister would get up and say "Be good" and point his finger and it always seemed like he was pointing at me. I used to think I knew what he meant, but now I don't. What is *good*, anyway?"

One of the more interesting aspects of Pamela's story has to do with the contradictory messages about sex she received while she was growing up. Her parents and her minister pronounced it wicked and sinful, yet she was never made to feel that masturbation was "bad," and her mother admitted to having had premarital intercourse. Contradictions are confusing, yet Pamela is one of the least confused of all the women I spoke with.

She recognizes sex as being important in the overall scheme of things, but that it is not life itself. She accepts herself to a degree that is unusual even among the ranks of sexually aggressive women: she's willing to try anything—trios, foursomes, sex with another woman, sex with a bisexual male. At the same time, she says with perfect candor that she must be masturbated to orgasm.

Like many of the younger women, she indicates a preference for a particular physical type; in her case, a tall, slender man with lots of hair. She is one of the few, however, who mention penis size as being important.

She has definite ideas about what she wants for the future: meaningful work, marriage—on her own terms—and children. She is sorting out her values, like all these young women, but finds her present life warm and loving and good. We should all be so lucky.

Chapter 5

THE MALE ANGLE

"... paradoxically, she who demands less will usually get more." So says an article in 1974 in the *Village Voice*, Greenwich Village's once-avant-garde weekly newspaper. The (male) writer is concerned. Worried. Impotence, it appears, is increasing and the sexually aggressive woman is to blame. She *uses* men, he says. Makes sex objects of them. It's not fair.

Charges of the same sort have appeared in *Esquire* and other periodicals. Worthy of note is a study by three New York psychiatrists that appeared in *Archives of General Psychiatry*. The authors' conclusion: that young men now appear in the offices of psychiatrists more frequently with problems of impotence, and that this is related to the female expecting orgastic release. *Psychology Today* polled its male readers about their experiences with impotence; one-third of the respondents reported having the problem, and female aggressiveness was implicated.

How ironic that this should happen just when great numbers of women—and not just the sexually aggressive, but many of the more passive and conventional as well—are waking up to their sexuality.

They are viewing it as a source of joy and pleasure instead of, as one married woman I know put it, "an obligation, something I avoid whenever I can," but the men are suddenly doing an about-face.

There is fear behind it all. Fear of not measuring up. When most women demanded nothing—not satisfaction, just "Get it over with, please"—most men felt very little pressure to perform. They *did* get it up and got it over with and were the all-around winners in a one-sided game.

Now women want to play the game, too, and men are confronted with the idea that there's more to the game than getting it up and over with.

(Perhaps it is unfortunate to use the game analogy. Good sex is not—cannot be—a competition. It is a cooperative venture: one gives to get. And usually, the more one gives, the more one gets. Many men and women would do well to keep this in mind.)

Classical psychoanalytical theories explain the dynamics of impotence, and though these theories undoubtedly apply in a great number of cases, it occurs to me that the impotence we're hearing about now may have something to do with men's feelings of guilt toward women. Sexually, and in other ways, too, men *have* used women—selfishly and often badly—and cannot help being aware of the fact at some level of consciousness. In which case, a whole chain of questions arises: After centuries of misuse, is woman finally getting *angry*? If she obtains the power she desires—again, sexually and in other areas—will there be a total turnabout? Will *she* become the user, and if so, will she—in the name of revenge—

use men as selfishly and badly as she herself was used?

These are questions I cannot answer. Revenge, like fear, takes many forms and is expressed in many ways. I can only say that although my interviews with sexually aggressive women were brief and although I acted as journalist rather than psychologist, I saw little evidence of man-hating or a desire for revenge in what they said. Their self-images are good, on the whole, and they act out of a simple desire to get what they want: more and better sex.

For them, male impotence, when it occurs, is a matter of disappointment, never a source of satisfaction. Although the Masters and Johnson study proved that women's sexual pleasure is independent of the penis—that orgasm through masturbation, use of a vibrator, or manual or oral stimulation by the partner is almost always more intense—by and large the women to whom I talked expressed a preference for the feeling of a penis inside them.

And, for whatever it's worth to the male whose insecurity stems in part from the dimensions of his penis, the majority of these "ultra-demanding" women were not especially concerned one way or another about size. All but the very smallest organs are felt within the vagina, which can, because of the elasticity of the vaginal walls, also stretch to accommodate all but the very largest. Far more important than the size of his penis is a man's understanding of how a particular woman is aroused, and the sexually aggressive woman will always show him.

Male impotence hardly figured in the testimonies

of the women with whom I spoke. I thought this might have happened because I was hearing only one side of the story. And so I decided to do a series of follow-up interviews with men.

I advertised for the men much as I had for the women. The respondents ranged in age from eighteen to sixty and represented a broad spectrum of educational, occupational, and economic backgrounds. Like the women, some were married, some single, some divorced, separated, or widowed. In all, I interviewed fifty men—only one of whom blamed his own periodic impotence on the sexual aggressiveness of his female partners.

In talking with these men, I was struck by their frankness and lack of inhibition, and I wonder if this is because sex talk has always come more naturally to the male than the female. That I was a woman seemingly created no problems—although some of the men, I'm sure, had the idea that in addition to being a journalist/psychologist, my interest also stamped me as a sex nut.

But whatever they may have thought of *me*, they almost all viewed the sexually aggressive woman with admiration and approval. They praised her openness, joyousness, freedom, and honesty. Some of the older men were especially appreciative.

"I feel I've been granted a bonus by living to see it happen," said a man in his fifties, commenting on the new sexual freedom of women.

A heavy-set forty-five-year-old trucking executive, divorced after twenty years of marriage, shook his head in apparent disbelief.

When I think of how hard I used to work to get a girl into the sack, and now that I'm just recently back in the action ... I can't believe it. They come after *me*. And everything. Oral sex when I was young was something only done by freaks. But not now!

Ronnie, a thirty-year-old bachelor, told this story:

Last year, for the first time, I met what you'd call a sexually aggressive woman. At a party. We got back to her apartment, and she asked me to lie down on the bed. Then she proceeded to take off my clothes. I said to myself, "Lie still and see what happens."

I did. I asked myself, "Why am I resenting it? Just because I'm not used to it, because I'm supposed to behave in a certain way because I'm male?"

She told me: "Now lie still and let me do it to you." She played with my cock and then began to suck me. Then I felt this strange feeling. The reversal turned me on. And I found myself being able to control my climax better than ever before. The enjoyment was incredible.

Who says the guy has to be aggressive? It was just—great sex.

Before that, I used to wear myself out dancing all night, spending half the time plotting how to get the girl into bed. Now, no games. This girl and I found ourselves talking straight, plain talk. It felt good. It's what I want from now on.

Brian, a twenty-one-year-old veteran of Vietnam, also told of initial resistance to female aggressiveness, which he overcame.

Last summer I was a lifeguard at a swim club and an older woman, close to forty I guess, was after me. I was too young and dumb to catch on.

She'd come to the pool just before closing time around nine at night and say, "Let's take a nude swim and I'll give you a ride home." Her daughter was nearly my age and it made me feel uncomfortable, so I said no. But I wanted to.

I guess I'm over that now because last week I met a girl and she said right out, "Hey, Brian, I'm horny, let's fuck." I smiled back at her and said, "Sure, Lucy. When and where?"

For Bob, a very blond and blue-eyed twenty-seven-year-old artist who came to New York from Kentucky, giving in to a sexually aggressive woman led to one of the most memorable experiences of his life.

I met this gal, Jan, at a coffee house. While we were having a drink together she told me she was a dancer and asked me to feel her thigh muscle, which was strong. After a few more minutes she asked me where I lived. I told her nearby, and she said, "Let's go there."

I tried to put her off at first. I didn't know who she was or what she was up to, but she kept urging me and telling me to feel her muscles, so finally I gave in.

When we got to my apartment, she took off her coat, grabbed me, pushed me down on the rug, and straddled me. Then she said something about how she knew karate and wrestling.

I began to struggle, but then she smiled, let me up, and kissed me. I could see that she was turned on. I decided to give in completely and see what would happen. By this time, she had taken off all my clothes and pushed me back on the rug again. She gave me a tongue bath all over my body, turned me on my back and then sucked me. Then she got on top and started pumping. I had one of the most overwhelming climaxes of my life.

When that was over, she took my hand, pulled me off the floor and said, "Let's go to bed."

In the bedroom she started in again, saying, "I'm going to show you how strong I am." She took one hand, put it on top of the other and held me down.

Then she wrapped her legs around my waist and squeezed hard. She said, "I'm going to do it to you again. Relax and take it easy." She began to play with my balls, then kissed them until I almost came.

Then she told me how to use my tongue on her clitoris. She liked alternating light and heavy licks . . . soft, then hard. This time she asked me to get on top.

When it was all over, we started talking. She

said she had a lover and she lived with him. She never gave me her address or phone number, but she's called me a couple of times since and invited herself over. That to me is one hell of a sexually aggressive woman.

And you know something? I did not feel demasculinized, even though all the time I was a little in awe of her.

On the other hand Ben, a tall, lean, sandy-haired twenty-nine-year-old television mechanic, has been unable to come to terms with female *social* aggressiveness, although he appreciates a certain forwardness in bed. Whether this is a manifestation of a blue-collar attitude I do not know. My sample was not large enough to tell; Ben in fact is not typically blue collar, either in the way he speaks or in his sensitivity to the subtleties of human relationships.

There's no kick when a woman gives in too easily. I like challenge. I want her to push me away several times and *then* give in. And not on the first date. I want to know something about her; I don't want to just hop into bed.

Yet Ben has no desire to carry any relationship to the point of marriage.

Some friends of mine just got back from their honeymoon in Acapulco. Know what they were doing? Swapping. On their *honeymoon!* I was an only child, my parents didn't play around, and if I should ever marry—which I doubt—I want to be faithful too. But there is just too much available to be faithful now.

In bed, anything and everything goes. Who wants to sleep with a board? The more action the better. A woman can play with me, lick me—anything. I'll do the same. Sex is lousy unless the woman is satisfied. And with an aggressive woman you feel *more* like a man, because her kicks are bigger.

Marty is a young man who likes *everything* about the sexually aggressive woman. He was born and grew up in a small town near Baltimore. He attended a nearby college, found it boring, and quit. He felt that New York was the place for him, so at twenty, he headed for the big city.

In the nearly ten years he has lived and worked there (mainly in photography studios), Marty has become an aficionado of the singles bars. He says he has had so many women that he has lost count, but one wonders, after hearing his story, if he has not been had by them.

What follows is only a part of his rambling account:

The women who work in New York hit the bars every night from five to nine. What else can they do? Especially those who are GU—geographically undesirable, hard to get to. They live in the Bronx or Brooklyn, away from the scene. What they want is a good dinner and a good lay.

The most fabulous scene is the stewardess scene. I met this stewardess named Meg one night in an East Side bar, and after we talked for an hour she invited me to live with her.

It was unbelievable. Nine girls sharing an apartment, but only a few of them there at any one time. Their men just kept coming through the door. Businessmen from all over just off the latest flight and in town for the night. Everyone getting laid, together or one to one. All the girls say they are looking for Mr. Right, and he's always going to be on the next plane.

After we'd balled the first time, Meg told me how she operated. She said she was a good amateur psychologist and knew which men would be turned on or off by her invitation. She told me the airlines know what's going on; they know, in New York especially, that for the stews, it's one big party after the landing. The younger gals in their twenties love it, but the older stews eventually get tired of it and ask to be transferred to a shuttle flight so they can get some sleep at home.

I stayed in that apartment two weeks, took a few turns with each of the girls. They'd invite me into their bedrooms whenever they felt like it. It was one of those giant old apartments with about six bedrooms, and it was a party day and night. Finally I couldn't take it anymore. Too much action, no privacy. In a way it was sad.

So I went back to the bars and, believe me, there's a bar for every taste in New York. . . .

There's one bar especially, where everyone,

men and women, dress in the most expensive clothes. Everyone has money and everyone wants to get laid.

But what's really different about this one is that the women are running the show. The men are studs, they flatter the women, but the women call the shots. They'll talk about the men in front of them and ask things like can they make it three or four times a night. It's a whole reverse-role bit. Guys thirty and up don't belong there. It's strictly a young twenties, money scene. . . .

From that bar scene, I wandered downtown to a bar where guys and gals go often and know each other. When a woman in this bar is looking for sex, she'll straddle the bar stool, the one you're sitting on, sort of like wrapping her legs around you.

I was sitting there one night and this gal walked in and said, "Joe broke up with me last night, so here I am, looking."

After a while she wandered over to me and invited me over to her pad. It was just around the corner, so I accepted. She took me in the bedroom, told me where to put my clothes, and the whole thing was over in half an hour. Then she turned over and looked at the clock. "My God," she said, "I didn't know it was so late. I'm expecting company. Can you get out quickly?" And it was already past midnight.

When I was younger I used to feel that if I went to bed with a woman she was going to be *mine*. Now it's just two bodies—you come, I come, that's all. The girls are out to ball, they find you, get you. It's different, but it's honest.

Marty, I'm afraid, is very much a young man adrift, a sad young man who has to get it together, to view his life from some new and wider perspective.

Bill, on the other hand, can deal with the sexually aggressive woman within the context of a satisfactorily structured life. He is a college instructor who wears the uniform of his profession—beard, pipe, worn tweed jacket with leather patches at the elbows—with casual ease and unselfconsciousness.

I don't have to get erections on call. I have moods, too, just like a woman. I understand some men can get it up at will, but not me. Even so, for ten years—I'm thirty-eight now—I've had sex every single day. You don't have to believe me but it's true. [I corroborated this statement with the woman who lives with him now, and it is true, at least for the last two years.]

I've had three primary women in my life. Between times I've masturbated. I must have the release, I don't feel comfortable unless I have it, but I'd never just pick up a woman.

A woman's sexual aggressiveness is what makes it fluid, beautiful. I want a woman who is a person and has her own career; so I can hardly expect her to turn off what she is in bed.

The woman I'm with now is the best. We talk a lot. She'll say, "What do you want? How?"

She uses her tongue delicately and sensitively.

If I'm eating her, she'll say "Lighter," or, "Great," or "Circle it"—that means the whole vaginal area. Or, "Too hard." Sometimes I press my tongue too hard against her clitoris. She tells me that actually takes away the feeling rather than increasing it.

I can't think of anything we haven't tried. Before she came along I never talked during sex. Just did it without conversation.

Sometimes she's dominant and climbs on top; I like it. I get a very special pleasure from just lying there, having her work on me. We respond and react, get enjoyment from everything; in this area I'm as much the pupil as the teacher.

Some men are always looking for quick lays. They actually like to hear a woman say, "Let's go to my place and get in some heavy breathing." A girl I met at a party recently said, "I've got cobwebs on my cunt." That really turned me off. In that sense I'm old-fashioned and feel it's almost sacrilegious to treat sex, which is truly beautiful when it's right, so mechanically.

All I can say is a woman has a right to be herself in bed, and when she is, she gives me more pleasure. Ego doesn't have a gender; it's a human word.

Bill's relationship with his friend is *almost* a marriage. John's *is* a marriage—and a happy one, according to this tall, handsome forty-year-old man.

My wife is sexually aggressive, and that's why our marriage works. No, I'll put it this way. We're both, say, seventy percent aggressive. One or the other of us is after the other to make love most of the time. I'm faithful by necessity, but also out of preference.

I work for a large building company with lots of girls in the steno pool. Sometimes I have to interview them for jobs. They come in wearing short dresses, open their knees so you can almost see their twats, and they flatter me. They say things like "You're a nice-looking guy," or, "I know I would enjoy working *under* you."

I know a few fellows who take a dip in the steno pool for extra refreshment; not me. I have all the action I want with my wife. Sure, women have been held down in business, and in sex. I've seen it for years. They're entitled to do their thing now. But by the same token, I want to do mine, and that happens to be to keep my marriage going as a happy, sexy establishment.

Word-for-word playbacks of all the interviews I conducted with these men would double the size of this volume. But I do want to include a few of their more significant comments beginning with some that indicate a positive attitude about the sexually aggressive woman:

- *She makes me feel sexier, more turned on.*
- *Because she's honest about her feelings, I feel I can be more honest with her—and that makes me feel better.*

- *She makes me want to satisfy her more.*
- *It's a whole new way of being with a woman—and a lot more fun.*
- *If a woman acts like she's doing you a favor in bed, what's the turn-on? If she wants what you want, then you're together.*
- *I hate games; that's why I relish the sexually aggressive woman. She doesn't play them.*
- *I enjoy her independence, socially and sexually.*
- *I like to get laid without a lot of phony conversation. So does she.*
- *I admire any person who can take care of himself—or herself. The sexually aggressive woman can.*
- *The more action in bed the better.*
- *When I'm tired after work I don't want to spend hours sparring with anybody. With a sexually aggressive woman you know right off whether you're in or out.*
- *Sex is a mutual satisfaction of needs. The sexually aggressive woman understands this. You don't have to go into hock unhappily ever after, just because you had a little fun.*
- *I find their frank use of words like "cock" and "pussy" turns me on more.*
- *Sexually aggressive women are stronger than other women. They have more orgasms.*

And finally this comment from an appreciative older man:

- *At fifty-five, it feels great to have a twenty-one-year-old without stretch marks come after me.*

Here are a few of the negative comments made about the sexually aggressive woman. Notice that most of them were made with reference to *social* aggressiveness, not necessarily against assertiveness in bed.

- *I don't like to be seduced when I'm not in the mood.*
- *O.K., she doesn't threaten me, but I'm the guy and I want to be the aggressor.*
- *I want the woman to see me as an individual, not a piece of meat.*
- *I don't like a woman to think she can make me an easy lay.*
- *Sex is personal to me. I like to feel that all the vibes are right before I hop into the sack with anybody.*
- *I don't like to hear a woman using words like "fuck" and "cock." It turns me off.*

The sexually aggressive woman obviously is not every man's ideal. I think it would be an error to conclude, even on the basis of fifty basically favorable opinions, that she is the ideal of *most* men. (Fifty men do not a population make.) Neither do I wish to excuse her entirely from contributing to what has been called the "new impotence" (which may, possibly, not be "new" at all, but merely the result of a new willingness to bring an age-old problem out into the open and to place it on the most convenient doorstep: woman's new sexual demands).

Whatever she is or isn't, or does or doesn't contribute to, she *is* an unsettling creature.

Women have had to hurdle several centuries' worth of man-made obstacles to gain some measure of sexual freedom. All during that time, the men were suffering, too—though in a different way. To simplify: papa put mama in the deepfreeze, because if she had functioned as a free, independent, sexual being, she would have been far less likely to hang around to keep *his* house, raise *his* children (not someone's else's bastards), and in general tend to *his* needs. But while mama sat there frozen—"good" and compliant but not sexy—what was papa to do about *his* unrepressed sexuality? He fashioned another woman, a passionate, uninhibited, forbidden creature, to meet his darker needs: the whore for the poor man, the courtesan or mistress for the rich.

So society's male leaders and thinkers came to live uneasily with the two kinds of women they had willed into being, the good but sexless wives, on the one hand, and the passionate but supposedly forbidden temptresses on the other.

Now women, no longer content to be shaped by the needs of men into one category or the other, are finding ways to will themselves into wholeness—sexual and "good" human beings who can live in the light as well as in darkness.

No wonder these new women—especially the sexually aggressive ones—are so provocative, even disturbing. No wonder that the men react with ambivalence. These women are shattering the very images that men, themselves, had shaped and grown to cherish.

I doubt that many women, once they've taken the first few steps toward wholeness, will be willing to go back, no matter how the men react. And so perhaps it is time for members of both sexes to relinquish their images of one another and learn to accept each other for what each has a right to be: an individual, whole human being.

club men themselves, had grown and grown and grown.

I doubt that any woman owns things other than her own soul...

About the Author

Adelaide Bry is a psychotherapist who, in addition to conducting a clinical practice, runs frequent workshops in transactional analysis for business groups.

She is a frequent guest on Philadelphia area radio and television shows, and has appeared nationally both with Mike Douglas and Johnny Carson.

In addition to THE SEXUALLY AGGRESSIVE WOMAN, New American Library has published Adelaide Bry's PRIMER OF BEHAVIORAL PSYCHOLOGY, INSIDE PSYCHOTHERAPY, and HOW TO GET ANGRY WITHOUT FEELING GUILTY.

⊘ **SIGNET**

FOR LOVERS ONLY

☐ **COLD FEET: WHY MEN WON'T COMMIT by Sonya Rhodes and Dr. Marlin S. Potash.** At last, a book for the thousands of intelligent and desirable women who find themselves drawing closer to a man—only to discover that just when things seem to be going great, he backs away and says he "needs more space." This groundbreaking book offers fascinating insight into the dynamics behind guys who both crave and fear intimacy—and tells you what you can do about it!
(159101—$4.50)

☐ **THE INNER MALE by Herb Goldberg.** A total re-evolution of problems faced by couples today with enlightening insights and compassionate solutions. Learn how to decode the mixed messages your partner can give ... learn to heal—without scarring—the wounds men's new sensitivity can create. "An insightful, creative analysis ... indispensable for both men and women."—Dr. Warren Farrell, *The Liberated Male* (156633—$4.95)

☐ **LOVE AND ADDICTION by Stanton Peele with Archie Brodsky.** This provocative book focuses on interpersonal relationships to explore what addiction really is—psychologically, socially, and culturally. "A rare book."—*Psychology Today* (155386—$4.95)

☐ **FOR EACH OTHER: Sharing Sexual Intimacy by Lonnie Barbach.** Every woman longs for greater sexual satisfaction and a more intimate relationship. Now this famed psychologist and sex therapist gives women a complete program for dealing with the complex aspects of a relationship—physical and psychological—that affect sexual satisfaction. (152719—$4.95)

☐ **MAKING LOVE: A WOMAN'S GUIDE by Judith Davis.** What does a man *really* want, anyway? You'll find all the answers in this one book that tells you how to turn your man on, including 20 sure-fire turn-ons to seduce him so he stays seduced; scores of gloriously imaginative ideas in the art of making love memorable; the well-known secret that kindles the steamiest sensual thrills; plus much, much more.
(155394—$4.50)

☐ **WOMEN MEN LOVE/WOMEN MEN LEAVE: WHAT MAKES MEN WANT TO COMMIT by Dr. Connell Cowan and Dr. Melvyn Kinder.** From the bestselling authors of *Smart Women, Foolish Choices* comes this indispensable guide to the puzzling patterns of a man's needs, fears, expectations and—yes!—commitment. Learn how to be a woman a man loves—and stays with—forever. (153065—$4.95)

Prices slightly higher in Canada

Buy them at your local bookstore or use this convenient coupon for ordering.

NEW AMERICAN LIBRARY
P.O. Box 999, Bergenfield, New Jersey 07621

Please send me the books I have checked above. I am enclosing $_____
(please add $1.00 to this order to cover postage and handling). Send check or money order—no cash or C.O.D.'s. Prices and numbers are subject to change without notice.

Name_____

Address_____

City _____ State _____ Zip Code _____
Allow 4-6 weeks for delivery.
This offer, prices and numbers are subject to change without notice.